# NODES OF WISDOM

## LESSONS FROM 100 CREATIVE VISIONARIES

## TEJJ

ISBN
Hardcase 979-8-89498-307-3
Paperback 979-8-89446-613-2

# Praises for Nodes of Wisdom: Lessons from 100 Creative Visionaries

*"A comprehensive design guide for both beginners and seasoned professionals, perfect for enhancing design skills for all backgrounds."*

*—Wolfgang Bremer, Design Executive,*
*Fortune 500s and Global Startups - Germany*

*"This book is a refreshingly straightforward collation of wisdom and experience from leading visionaries on creative excellence. As a podcast host, Tejj has done what is relevant for our times; distilling the conversations and sharing takeaways with a broader audience through writing. Such a treasure trove of diverse perspectives, engaging storytelling, and practical advice to enhance your creative process. I highly recommend this book to anyone seeking to widen their perspectives or revisit the fundamentals of creative excellence; starting with deep inquiry and empathy and navigating into forward-looking innovative thinking around AI."*

*—Gloria Osardu, PhD,*
*Global Head of Research and Insights Gusto, Inc - USA*

*Nodes of Wisdom goes beyond mere discussions about design as it deeply dives into the essence of community collaboration and enthusiastic participation. Every section illuminates the path to a deeper understanding of fundamental design principles and celebrates the collective spirit and inherent wisdom of the community. Through engaging narratives and inspiring case studies, Tejj captures the magic that occurs when individuals from diverse backgrounds and skills come together with a common purpose. This book is a powerful testament to how collaboration and active participation can lead to extraordinary outcomes, not just in the field of design but in any creative endeavour. It is a must-read for those seeking to understand the true value of community in creation and innovation.*

**—Rafael Brandão, Director,
Product Experience LATAM, Warner Bros.
Discovery - Brazil**

*Tejj has distilled his conversations with creative leaders and has presented them back as a comprehensive yet approachable overview of some of the best principles and approaches to creativity and design. Covering foundational principles like empathy, storytelling, and leading with purpose, to how current and future technologies can augment and shift how we approach creativity, Nodes of Wisdom offers insights not just for new and seasoned creatives, but for anyone with the curiosity to create. As Tejj says - "Empathy is more than just a buzzword; it's a fundamental approach that can elevate our designs from functional to meaningful." This book could have been very functional, simply listing processes and standard principles easily found online, but because he has taken the time to engage with industry leaders, listen to what they have to say, this book is meaningful and a worthwhile read.*

**—Iain McConchie, Senior Director of Design & Product, ChowNow - USA**

*The best learnings and insights come from your own experiences. "Nodes of Design" features a collection of over 100 interviews with industry experts who share their wisdom through personal journeys, success stories, and lessons learned from failures. Other designers can draw valuable insights from these narratives. I love the idea of crafting a book based on these learnings!*

*Every chapter of "Nodes of Wisdom" guides readers through essential design themes like empathy, storytelling, resilience, and innovation. The book skillfully intertwines visionary interviews, presenting a holistic guide that enhances creative practice and enriches personal growth. It's an indispensable resource for designers looking to deepen their craft and build meaningful connections.*

**—Riya Thosar, Director of Product Design, SAP - USA**

*Nodes of Design is already an inspiring podcast, but the book is absolutely unmissable. It captures the essence of what it takes to be a fulfilled creative professional. Its structure highlights the core transferable skills of a successful designer. It is an inspiration based on real experiences, real stories, of real people. It shows how a person like you and me can create their unique journey to success. It demonstrates how ordinary people* can create innovative and meaningful products and services that reach people's unmet needs and desires, regardless of their physical or mental abilities. It's an opportunity to become a better designer but also, and most importantly, a better person.

**—Denise Pilar, Professor of UX Research and Design at SCAD - Savannah College of Art and Design, in Savannah, GA - USA**

"When I first met Ravi Tej, being invited for the Nodes of Design podcast, I was fascinated by the meticulous details he took care of in his podcast. From sound quality to world class editing. Ever since the podcast has been a bookmarked gem in my audio library.

Nodes of Wisdom is another such gem which is handcrafted and almost acts like an offline mentor for students and professionals alike.

His chapters delve into the heart of empathy, the craft of compelling narratives, and the mastery of fundamental design principles, offering readers a well-rounded foundation for creating impactful work.

Tej's insights into the intersection of art and design, the creation of inclusive experiences, and the exciting new frontiers opened by AI and immersive realities, make this work an indispensable resource for students and professionals. This book is a must have in libraries across colleges and corporates."

**—Amit Patil, Principal Design Manager, Microsoft, India**

*Nodes of Wisdom by Tej provides an important foundation on the design practice, and it goes much further, by empowering creative professionals with a set of strategies to thrive in a challenging, competitive, and fast-paced world.*

**—Manuel Lima, Interos.ai,
Senior Product Design Director, USA**

*Most books on creativity make you choose between inspiration and practical insights. That's not the case with this book. It draws from hundreds of interviews with some of the world's most talented people, and Tejj excels at turning complex concepts into actionable insights. Every creative, whether junior or senior, should read this.*

**—Anton Sten, Head of Design, Summer Health**

*Tejj has woven together a wealth of wisdom from his insightful interviews with creative geniuses, design masters, and UX pioneers. This book is a powerful resource, distilling their knowledge into a must-read for anyone seeking to elevate their craft.*

**—Rich McCoy, Freelance product
design director at McCoy and Co.**

*This book is like a journey through the back alleys and hidden gems of the design world. It dives deep into the minds of the world's top creatives, offering unique insights and strategies that are as enlightening as a late-night conversation over a good meal.*

*Tejj covers it all—from how empathy can fuel innovation and storytelling can breathe life into data, to how resilience can turn setbacks into stepping stones. And let's not forget the latest tech—AI, AR, and VR—it's all in there.*

*I've been designing remotely with my agency, working with heavyweights like Google, Apple, Marriott, and NBC Universal. Trust me, this book captures the essence of what makes design truly exceptional. Whether you're a newbie or a seasoned pro, "Nodes of Wisdom" offers a treasure trove of inspiration and practical advice.*

**—Sharif Matar, UX Design Director, Product Inc**

*In "Nodes of Wisdom," Ravi Tejj has distilled down a plethora of insights gleaned from 100s of conversations with design industry leaders — each node leaving readers inspired, delighted, educated, and with the belief that design and storytelling have the power to transcend. Whether you're a student of design or a seasoned expert, you're guaranteed to pick up not only practical tools and frameworks but also some profound design (and life!) wisdom from this book.*

**—Kristen Shenk, Founder + Creative Director,
MLTI NYC and The Mindful Creative**

*A treasure house of on ground case studies to touch every aspect of design + nodes of wisdom from design leaders. It's unmissable!!*

**—Ekta Rohra Jafri, APAC Design Leader,
Srijan- A Material+ Company**

*This book is a masterful distillation of wisdom from top global creative minds from the renowned Nodes of Design podcast, offering insights and stories that span empathy in design, storytelling, and creativity. From personal to global, each chapter serves as an inspiring guide for emerging or practicing designers. This book shows us design as it is understood and practiced now.*

**—Ruki Neuhold-Ravikumar**
**Design Strategist & Leadership Consultant,**
**arc c.suite advisory, USA**

# Dedication

This book is dedicated to my mother and father, whose unwavering love and guidance have been the cornerstone of my journey and to my family, who have always stood by me, offering their endless support and encouragement.

To all my mentors, who have shared their wisdom, inspired my growth, and believed in my potential even when I doubted myself.

And to every person who has prayed for me, blessed me, and sent positive thoughts my way—your kindness and faith have been the invisible hand that has guided me through every challenge and triumph.

This book is a testament to the power of blessings, love, and the profound impact of a supportive community. Thank you for enabling me to share these lessons and insights with the world.

# Disclaimer

Please note that the information contained in this document is for educational and entertainment purposes only. While all efforts have been made to present accurate, up-to-date, reliable, and complete information, no warranties of any kind are declared or implied. The content within this book has been derived from various sources and transcripts from Nodes of Design Podcast.

By reading this document, readers agree that under no circumstances is the author responsible for any direct or indirect losses incurred as a result of the use of the information contained within this document, including but not limited to errors, omissions, or inaccuracies.

# Contents

# Introduction

## Welcome to Nodes of Wisdom

Welcome to "Nodes of Wisdom: Lessons from 100 Creative Visionaries." If you've ever found yourself in awe of a brilliantly designed product, captivated by a moving piece of art, or inspired by a story of perseverance, then this book is for you. This book is a labour of love, born out of countless conversations with some of the creative industry's most brilliant and inspiring minds. Over the years, I've had the privilege of hosting the "Nodes of Design" podcast, where I've interviewed design leaders, artists, researchers, and visionaries worldwide. Each episode has been a treasure trove of insights, and I'm thrilled to share these lessons with you.

As a designer, mentor, and design evangelist, I've always been passionate about understanding what drives creativity and innovation. Through these conversations, I've discovered that the journey of a creative professional is filled with unique experiences, challenges, and triumphs. This book aims to capture those stories and distil the wisdom gathered from them into practical advice and inspiration for your creative journey.

## The Power of Design Stories

Stories have an incredible power to inspire, teach, and connect us. They are the threads that weave together our experiences and insights into a cohesive narrative. In the realm of design, stories play a crucial role in conveying complex ideas, evoking emotions, and driving meaningful change.

Throughout this book, you will find stories highlighting the importance of empathy, the art of storytelling, the significance of mastering fundamental principles, and the transformative power of curiosity and data. These stories are not just about design; they are about life. They illustrate how creativity can be harnessed to solve problems, create beauty, and connect people.

I strongly believe Design is not just about making things look good; it's about making things work, meaningful, and impactful. The stories and lessons shared in this book reflect this holistic view of design, emphasising its potential to influence and improve every aspect of our lives.

## Who is this book for?

This book is for every creative soul, whether you are a student, a seasoned professional, or simply curious about designing beautiful and impactful products. It's for anyone who wants to dive deep into the design world, gain insights from leading visionaries, and discover the timeless principles and cutting-edge techniques that shape extraordinary creations. No matter where you are in your design journey, this book will inspire, guide, and empower you to reach new heights in your creative endeavours.

## The Structure of This Book

"Nodes of Wisdom" is organised into sixteen chapters, each focusing on a different aspect of the creative process and the life lessons learned from the visionaries I've had the pleasure and honour of interviewing. The chapters are designed to flow logically, building on each other to provide a comprehensive guide to enhancing your creative practice.

### Chapter 1: The Heart of Empathy

Empathy is the foundation of effective design. We will explore how understanding the needs, emotions, and experiences of others can transform your design process and enrich your personal life.

### Chapter 2: Crafting Compelling Narratives

Storytelling is a powerful tool for conveying ideas and inspiring action. Here, we root into techniques for turning data into compelling stories and how personal journeys can resonate with audiences.

### Chapter 3: Mastering the Timeless Fundamentals

While tools and technologies change, the fundamental principles of design remain constant. Here, we emphasise mastering these basics to create timeless and impactful designs.

## Chapter 4: Curiosity Unleashed

Curiosity drives innovation. This chapter highlights the importance of maintaining a curious mindset and balancing curiosity with action to foster continuous learning and creativity.

## Chapter 5: Guiding Lights: Mentorship and Community

Mentorship and community are crucial for growth and development. Here we discuss finding the right mentors, building supportive communities, and leveraging these relationships for personal and professional growth.

## Chapter 6: Resilience: Standing Up and Facing Defeat

Every creative journey encounters setbacks and failures. This chapter focuses on building resilience, learning from failures, and developing the strength to persevere in facing challenges.

## Chapter 7: The Gift of Feedback: Receiving and Growing

Feedback is essential for growth and improvement. Here, we discuss embracing feedback as a valuable tool, providing constructive criticism, and effectively incorporating feedback into your work.

## Chapter 8: Crafting Your Legacy: Building a Personal Brand as a Designer

A solid personal brand is essential for designers to stand out and advance their careers in a competitive market.

This chapter explores the importance of personal branding and offers strategies for defining your brand identity, creating a professional online presence, sharing your expertise, and engaging authentically with your audience.

## Chapter 9: Leading with Purpose: Design Leadership and Values

Leadership in design goes beyond managing projects; it's about inspiring and guiding teams to create meaningful work. Here we dive into the core values of design leadership, building effective teams, and fostering a culture of innovation.

## Chapter 10: The Intersection of Art and Design: Blurring the Lines

Art and design often intersect, creating a dynamic creative landscape. This chapter discusses how artistic principles can enhance design practice and the benefits of interdisciplinary collaboration.

## Chapter 11: Designing for All: Creating Inclusive Experiences

Designing for accessibility ensures that products and services are usable by everyone, regardless of their abilities. Here, we explore the principles of accessible design, practical strategies for creating inclusive experiences, and the benefits of prioritising accessibility.

## Chapter 12: Designing Beyond Screens: Expanding Horizons

Design is not confined to digital screens. Here we take a look at the principles and practices of designing physical products, spatial experiences, and environmentally responsible designs.

## Chapter 13: The Art and Science of Data-Driven Design

Data is a powerful tool for informing design decisions. This chapter explores integrating data into your design process, creating impactful visualisations, and leveraging data for deeper insights.

## Chapter 14: AI and the Creative Process: A New Frontier

Artificial Intelligence is revolutionising the design industry. Here, we examine how AI can enhance creativity, the ethical considerations it raises, and its practical applications in design.

## Chapter 15: Immersive Realities: AR, VR, and Intelligent Interfaces

The future of design lies in immersive realities and intelligent interfaces. This chapter explores the potential of AR and VR, the advancements in intelligent interfaces, and practical tips for designing these new realities.

## Chapter 16: The Business of Design: Balancing Creativity and Commerce

Mastering the business side of design is crucial for success. This chapter talks about aligning design with business goals, effective pricing strategies, financial literacy, and the importance of building strong client relationships. Practical frameworks and real-world examples guide designers in balancing creativity with commerce to ensure sustainable growth and profitability.

## A Journey Through Creativity

As you embark on this journey through the pages of "Nodes of Wisdom," I encourage you to approach each chapter with an open mind and a willingness to explore new ideas. Whether you are a seasoned designer, a budding creative, or someone simply curious about the world of design, this book is for you.

Each chapter is filled with practical advice, thought-provoking insights, and inspiring stories that will challenge you to think differently about your work and life. The lessons shared here are not just theoretical; they are grounded in real-world experiences and tested by some of the best minds in the industry.

I hope this book will be a source of inspiration and a guide for your creative journey. May it encourage you to push the boundaries of your creativity, embrace empathy and curiosity, and create work that is not only beautiful but also meaningful and impactful.

## The Nodes of Design Podcast

The "Nodes of Design" podcast has been a platform for exploring the diverse perspectives and experiences of creative professionals. Through these interviews, I've had the opportunity to dive deep into the minds of visionaries, learning about their processes, challenges, and triumphs.

The podcast has taught me that creativity is a journey filled with obstacles and opportunities. It has shown me that the best ideas often come from unexpected places and that the most successful creatives are those who are willing to take risks, fail, and learn from their failures.

In this book, I've distilled the essence of these conversations, extracting the key lessons and insights that can benefit anyone on their creative journey. While the podcast provided the foundation, this book aims to build upon it, offering a more comprehensive and structured exploration of the themes and lessons discussed.

## The Visionaries Behind the Wisdom

The visionaries featured in the podcast come from diverse backgrounds and disciplines, each bringing their unique perspectives and experiences. They are design leaders, artists, researchers, and thought leaders who have made significant contributions to their fields. While their paths may differ, they all share a common thread: a passion for creativity and a commitment to making a positive impact through their work.

Their stories are a testament to the power of perseverance, the importance of empathy, and the transformative potential of creativity. By sharing their journeys, they offer valuable lessons that can inspire and guide you on your path.

## How to Use This Book

"Nodes of Wisdom: Lessons from 100 Creative Visionaries" is designed to be both a guide and a source of inspiration. Each chapter can be read independently, allowing you to focus on the areas that resonate most with you. However, I encourage you to read the entire book to fully appreciate the interconnectedness of the lessons and themes.

Take your time with each chapter, reflecting on the insights and considering how they apply to your work and life. Use the practical tips and exercises to experiment with new approaches and deepen your understanding of the concepts discussed.

Above all, let this book be your companion on your creative journey. I believe you will always return to it whenever you need inspiration, guidance, or a reminder of the wisdom shared by the creative visionaries who have contributed to its pages.

## Final Thoughts

As we embark on this journey together, I want to express my gratitude to all the visionaries who have generously shared their stories and insights. Their contributions have made this book possible, and their wisdom inspires me daily.

Thank you, the reader, for joining me on this adventure. It is your curiosity and passion for creativity that drives us all forward. This book will ignite your imagination, fuel your creativity, and empower you to make a meaningful impact through your work.

Welcome to "Nodes of Wisdom." Let's begin this journey of discovery and inspiration together.

# CHAPTER 1

## The Heart of Empathy

Empathy is the beating heart of great design. It is an invisible thread that connects us to our users, enabling us to create experiences that resonate deeply with their needs, desires, and emotions. As a designer, mentor, and design evangelist, I've seen firsthand the transformative power of empathy in the creative process. This chapter delves into the essence of empathy, how it enriches our work, and why it is an indispensable tool for any creative professional.

### Embracing Empathy in Design

Empathy is more than just a buzzword; it's a fundamental approach that can elevate our designs from functional to meaningful. When we design with empathy, we step into our users' shoes, understanding their world from their perspective. This shift in viewpoint allows us to address their real problems, not just the symptoms.

One of my most memorable experiences was working with a team building a healthcare app. We spent days in hospitals, observing and interacting with patients, doctors, and nurses. The more time we spent with them, the more we understood the emotional highs and lows they experienced daily. It wasn't just about managing appointments or tracking medications. It was about the anxiety patients felt while waiting for test results, the stress nurses faced managing their time, and the compassion doctors showed while delivering difficult news. These insights helped us design experiences that mattered to these users and were only possible because we immersed ourselves in their world, empathising with their experiences.

To truly embrace empathy in design, we must cultivate a curiosity and openness mindset. This means being genuinely interested in the lives of others, asking questions, and listening with intent. It involves conducting user research, not as a checkbox activity but as a journey to uncover our users' nuanced needs and desires. It means observing how people interact with our designs or systems in their natural environments and understanding the context in which they use them.

## Practical Empathy: Methods and Approaches

One of the most effective ways to build empathy is through user interviews. Sitting down with users and conversing about their experiences can reveal insights that no amount of analytics can provide. These conversations should be open-ended and exploratory, allowing users to express their thoughts and feelings freely. Questions like, "Can you tell me about a time when you faced a challenge with this product?" or "What emotions did you feel when using this feature?" can open doors to deeper understanding.

Consider the case of a design team working on a new educational app for children. By interviewing parents, teachers, and students, they discovered that while parents were concerned about screen time, teachers were more focused on educational outcomes, and students simply wanted to have fun. This nuanced understanding led to a design that balanced educational content with engaging, interactive elements, addressing the needs of all stakeholders.

Another powerful method is shadowing, where you observe users in their natural environment as they interact with your product or service. This approach helps you see the world through their eyes, understand their workflows, and identify pain points that might surface outside of an interview setting. For instance, shadowing a group of factory workers using a new inventory system might reveal inefficiencies and frustrations that would be missed in a more formal setting.

Empathy mapping is a visual tool that helps consolidate what you've learned about your users. It involves creating a detailed profile of your user, including their thoughts, feelings, pains, and gains. This map becomes a reference point throughout the design process, ensuring that your decisions remain user-centred.

## Empathy Map

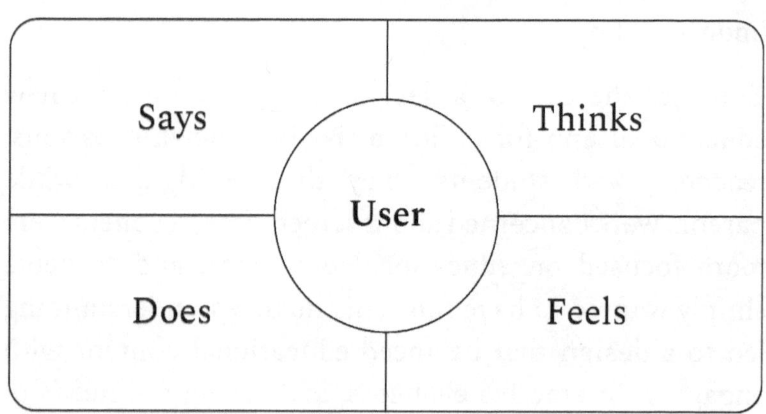



An empathy map helped a team redesign a public transportation app in one project. By capturing the anxiety, frustration, and confusion experienced by users, they identified critical areas for improvement, such as real-time updates and more precise navigation. This user-centred approach led to a significant increase in user satisfaction and adoption rates.

## Empathy in Life

Empathy extends beyond the confines of our professional lives. It's a skill that enriches our personal relationships and makes us better people. In our daily interactions, empathy allows us to connect with others on a deeper level, fostering understanding and compassion.

In one of my podcast interviews, a seasoned researcher emphasised, "Empathy is not just about understanding others; it's about valuing their experiences as much as your own." This perspective is transformative. When we value others' experiences, we create a culture of respect and inclusion. We become more attuned to the emotional landscapes of our friends, family, and colleagues, leading to stronger and more meaningful connections.

Practising empathy in our personal lives also makes us better designers. When we are attuned to the human condition, we bring a richer, more nuanced perspective to our work. We become more adept at anticipating the needs of our users and designing solutions that truly resonate with them.

I remember a particular story shared by a guest on my podcast, a renowned designer who spoke about how his mother's struggle with arthritis influenced his design approach. Watching her struggle with everyday tasks inspired him to create products that were not only functional but also accessible and easy to use. This personal connection to empathy drove him to design with a deeper purpose, ensuring his products made a real difference in people's lives.

## Empathy in Action: Real-World Examples

One of the most compelling examples of empathy in design comes from the world of healthcare. A design team working on a new hospital system spent weeks shadowing doctors, nurses, and patients. They observed the daily routines, interactions and challenges each group faced. This immersive research revealed that one of the most significant pain points for patients was the need for more transparent communication about their treatment plans.

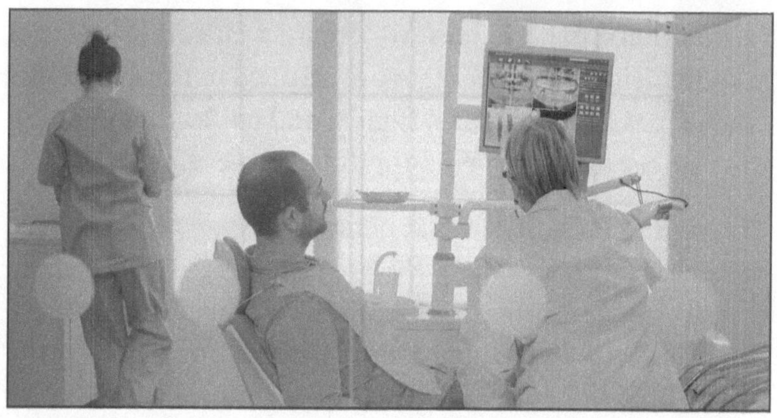

Armed with this insight, the design team developed a simple yet powerful solution: a digital dashboard that provided real-time updates on treatment plans, test results, and scheduled procedures. This dashboard not only improved the patient experience but also enhanced the workflow for healthcare providers. By designing with empathy, the team created a solution that addressed the needs of all stakeholders.

In another instance, a tech company building a new mobile app for seniors took a different approach. Instead of relying solely on data analytics, they conducted in-home visits with elderly users. They discovered that many seniors needed help with small text sizes and complex navigation structures. These insights led to the development of an app with larger text, simplified navigation, and voice-assisted commands, making it more accessible and user-friendly for older adults.

## Practical Tips for Building Empathy

**Engage with Users:** Spend time with your users, observe their interactions, and listen to their stories. This direct engagement will give you invaluable insights that data alone can't provide.

**Avoid Assumptions:** Approach each project with a fresh perspective, free of preconceived notions. Assumptions can cloud your judgement and lead to many revisions.

**Practise Active Listening:** Pay attention to both verbal and non-verbal cues during user interactions. Sometimes, the most important insights are found in what users don't say explicitly.

**Conduct Immersive Research:** Immerse yourself in the environments where your users interact with your product. This firsthand experience will deepen your understanding and reveal context-specific challenges.

**Walk in Their Shoes:** Whenever possible, experience the product or service from the user's perspective. Use the same tools, follow the same processes, and see how it feels. This can reveal pain points and opportunities for improvement that you might otherwise miss.

## The Transformative Power of Empathy

Empathy is not a static skill; it's a dynamic force that evolves with practice and intention. As we develop our ability to empathise, we become better designers and people. We learn to see the world through multiple lenses, appreciating the diversity of human experience.

Incorporating empathy into your design process is not just about creating better products; it's about making a positive impact on the lives of others. When we design with empathy, we create solutions that are not only functional but also meaningful and impactful. We move from designing for users to designing with them, fostering a collaborative spirit that leads to innovation and excellence.

Empathy also empowers us to challenge our biases and assumptions. It encourages us to question the status quo and seek diverse perspectives. This openness to different viewpoints enriches our work and creates more inclusive and equitable designs.

## Empathy: The Heartbeat of Innovation

Empathy is the heartbeat of innovation. It drives us to explore new possibilities and create solutions that truly resonate with our users. By putting ourselves in others' shoes, we unlock a deeper understanding of their needs and desires, paving the way for breakthroughs that might otherwise remain out of reach.

One visionary I interviewed said, "Innovation starts with empathy and it is the spark that ignites creativity and is the foundation upon which great designs are built." This sentiment encapsulates the essence of empathy in the creative process. It propels us to look beyond the obvious and explore the deeper layers of human experience.

Consider the story of a startup working on wearable technology for athletes. By empathising with the athletes' needs, the team discovered it wasn't just about tracking performance metrics. The athletes needed real-time feedback to prevent injuries and optimise their training.

This insight led to the development of a wearable device that not only tracked data but also provided actionable insights and alerts, helping athletes train smarter and safer.

## The Journey of Empathy

The journey of empathy is one of continuous growth and learning. It requires us to be humble, open-minded, and willing to listen. It's about recognising that we don't have all the answers and that the best solutions often come from understanding the experiences of others.

One of the most inspiring stories of empathy in action comes from education. A group of designers working on a new learning platform spent months in classrooms, observing teachers and students. They discovered that while technology could enhance learning, the human connection between teachers and students made the most significant difference. This insight led them to design a platform that supported and amplified these human connections rather than replacing them. The result was a tool that empowered teachers, engaged students, and improved learning outcomes.

In another project, a financial services company aimed to design a new budgeting app for millennials. They conducted extensive interviews and surveys to understand this demographic's financial habits and challenges. They discovered that many young adults were overwhelmed by the complexity of financial management and desired a more straightforward, more intuitive solution. Using this empathy-driven insight, the company built an app that simplified budgeting, provided personalised financial advice, and used gamification to make financial management engaging and rewarding.

## The Empathic Designer's Toolkit

Empathy is a multifaceted skill that can be cultivated through various practices and approaches. Here are some essential tools and techniques for building and enhancing empathy in your design process:

**User Personas:** Creating detailed user personas based on accurate user data helps you visualise and understand your target audience's needs, goals, and pain points. These personas are a reference throughout the design process, ensuring your solutions remain user-centred.

**Journey Mapping:** Mapping out the user journey helps you identify critical touchpoints, pain points, and opportunities for improvement. This visual representation of the user's experience provides a comprehensive view of how they interact with your product or service over time.

**Contextual Inquiry:** Conducting contextual inquiries involves observing and interviewing users in their natural environment. This method allows you to gain a deeper understanding of the user's context, behaviours, and challenges, providing valuable insights for your design.

**Co-Design Workshops:** Involving users in the design process through co-design workshops and sessions fosters collaboration and ensures their voices are heard. These workshops allow users to contribute ideas, provide feedback, and participate in creating solutions.

**Emotional Mapping:** Mapping out the emotional journey of your users helps you understand their feelings and emotions at different stages of their interaction with your product or service. This insight enables you to design experiences that resonate on an emotional level.

## The Ripple Effect of Empathy

Empathy has a ripple effect that extends beyond the immediate design process. When we design with empathy, we create products and services that positively impact society. We contribute to a culture of understanding, compassion, and inclusivity.

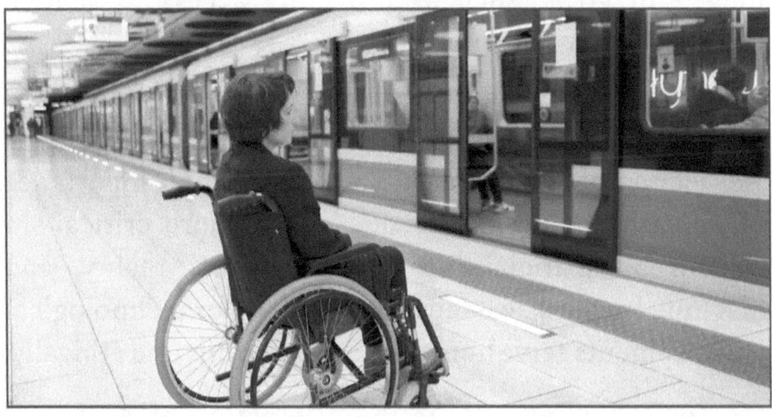

Consider the example of a community organisation working to improve public transportation in a major city. By engaging with diverse groups of users, including people with disabilities, elderly residents, and low-income families, the organisation gained a holistic understanding of the transportation challenges faced by different segments of the population. This empathy-driven approach led to the establishment of a more inclusive and accessible public transportation system that improved the quality of life for all residents.

Empathy also plays a crucial role in addressing complex social issues. For instance, a design team working on a project to combat homelessness conducted in-depth interviews with individuals experiencing homelessness, social workers, and community advocates. By empathising with the lived experiences of those affected, the team gained valuable insights into the systemic barriers and challenges the homeless population faces. This understanding informed the design of innovative solutions that addressed both immediate needs and long-term goals, such as providing access to shelter, healthcare, and job opportunities.

## Empathy in the Age of Technology

As technology continues to evolve, the importance of empathy in design becomes even more critical. In an era of artificial intelligence, virtual reality, and machine learning, we must ensure that our technological advancements serve humanity meaningfully and ethically.

One powerful example is the origination of AI-driven mental health support tools. By empathising with individuals experiencing mental health challenges, designers and researchers have created AI-powered chatbots that provide emotional support, resources, and referrals to mental health professionals. These tools offer a valuable complement to traditional mental health services, making support more accessible to those in need.

Similarly, the rise of virtual reality (VR) has opened new avenues for empathy-driven design. VR experiences that simulate the perspectives of individuals with different abilities, backgrounds, or life experiences can foster greater understanding and empathy among users.

For example, VR simulations that enable users to experience the challenges faced by people with disabilities can raise awareness and promote more inclusive design practices.

## The Empathic Design Leader

As designers, we have the opportunity to lead by example and champion empathy within our organisations and communities. Empathic design leadership involves creating an environment where empathy is valued, practised, and integrated into every aspect of the design process.

Empathic leaders prioritise listening and understanding. They create spaces where team members feel safe to share their ideas, experiences, and concerns. They encourage open dialogue and actively seek out diverse perspectives, recognising that innovation thrives in an environment of inclusivity and respect.

In one organisation, a design leader implemented regular "empathy sessions" where team members shared stories and insights from their user research. These sessions fostered a culture of empathy, collaboration, and continuous learning, leading to more user-centred and impactful design outcomes.

Empathic design leaders also advocate for user-centred decision-making at all levels of the organisation. They ensure user insights and feedback are integrated into strategic planning, product development, and evaluation processes. By championing empathy, they inspire others to prioritise users' needs and experiences, ultimately creating a more human-centred and impactful design practice.

## Conclusion: The Empathic Designer

Empathy is the heart of great design. It's the foundation upon which we build meaningful, impactful, and innovative solutions. By embracing empathy, we open ourselves to a world of insights and opportunities that can transform our work and lives.

As you continue your journey as a designer, remember that empathy is your most vital tool. Cultivate it, nurture it, and let it guide you. Embrace your users' stories, value their experiences, and design with their needs at the forefront. In doing so, you'll create work that meets the functional requirements and touches the hearts and minds of those interacting with it.

Empathy is the thread that connects us all. It's the force that drives us to understand, innovate, and create. By putting empathy at the heart of our design process, we can positively impact the world and create experiences that truly matter.

So, let empathy be your guiding star. Let it illuminate your path and inspire you to create with compassion, curiosity, and a deep understanding of the human experience. The journey of empathy is ongoing, and it starts with you.

# CHAPTER 2

## Crafting Compelling Narratives

Stories are the lifeblood of human connection. They have the power to inspire, teach, and move us. In design, storytelling is a powerful tool that allows us to convey complex ideas, evoke emotions, and drive meaningful change. This chapter explores the art of crafting compelling narratives, offering frameworks and techniques to enhance your storytelling in your work and portfolio. Whether you're presenting a design concept, sharing user research, or showcasing your work, storytelling can elevate your message and resonate deeply with your audience.

### The Power of Stories in Design

At its core, design is about communication. It's about conveying a message, solving a problem, and creating an experience. Stories provide a framework for this communication, making abstract concepts tangible and relatable. They help us understand the world and our place in it. When we weave stories into our design process, we create a narrative that our audience can connect with, understand, and remember.

Imagine presenting a new app design to a client. Instead of merely listing features, you tell the story of "Mira," a busy working mother who struggles to find time for herself. You describe how the app helps Mira manage her schedule, find moments of calm, and connect with her family. This narrative transforms your presentation from a dry list of functionalities into a compelling story highlighting the app's value and impact.

## The Anatomy of a Compelling Story

A compelling story has a clear structure that guides the audience through a journey. This structure typically includes the following elements:

**The Hook:** To capture your audience's attention, start with an intriguing question, a surprising fact, or a relatable scenario.

**The Setting:** Provide context for your story by describing the environment, the characters, and the situation. This helps your audience visualise and relate to the story.

**The Conflict:** Introduce the main challenge or problem that must be solved. This creates tension and engages your audience, making them invested in the outcome.

**The Resolution:** Describe how the challenge is overcome and the problem is solved. Highlight the solution and its impact on the characters and the situation.

**The Takeaway:** End with a clear message or lesson that reinforces the story's purpose and leaves a lasting impression on your audience.

## Storytelling Frameworks for Design

To craft compelling narratives in your work and portfolio, consider using the following storytelling frameworks:

### The Hero's Journey

The Hero's Journey, popularised by Joseph Campbell, is a universal storytelling structure that can be applied to design narratives. It follows a hero who embarks on an adventure, faces challenges, and returns transformed. Here's how you can use this framework in your design storytelling:

### The Hero's Journey

- **The Call to Adventure:** Introduce the problem or opportunity that prompts the hero (user) to take action. Describe their initial situation and the motivation for change.

- **The Journey:** Detail the user's journey as they interact with your design. Highlight their challenges and how your design helps them overcome them.

- **The Transformation:** Show your design's positive impact on the user's life. Describe the improvements, benefits and overall transformation.

For example, if you're showcasing a new fitness app, your hero could be "James", who struggles to maintain a healthy lifestyle. The call to adventure is James' realisation that he needs to get fit. The journey involves James using the app to track his workouts, stay motivated, and overcome challenges. Through the app, James's health and confidence have been transformed.

## The STAR Framework (Situation, Task, Action, Result)

The STAR framework is a simple yet effective structure for telling stories, particularly in professional contexts. It involves describing the Situation, the Task at hand, the Action taken, and the Result achieved. STAR framework can be used to present case studies, design projects, and user research.

**The STAR Framework**

Situation    Task    Action    Result

**Situation:** Describe the context and background of the project or problem. What was the initial situation? Who were the stakeholders involved?

**Task:** Define the task or goal. What needed to be achieved? What were the goals and expectations?

**Action:** Detail the actions you took to address the task. What design decisions did you make? What methods and tools did you use?

**Result:** Highlight the results and outcomes of your actions. What was the impact of your design? How did it solve the problem or improve the situation?

For instance, if you're presenting a website redesign, you might describe the initial situation (a cluttered and outdated website), the task (modernising the design and improving user experience), the actions taken (user research, wireframing, prototyping), and the results (a user-friendly website with increased engagement and positive feedback).

## The Pixar Pitch

The Pixar Pitch is a storytelling technique Pixar uses to create compelling movie narratives. It follows a simple structure that can be adapted for design storytelling:

- **Once upon a time:** Set the scene and introduce the characters and context.

- **Every day:** Describe the normal world and routine of the characters.

- **One day:** Introduce the inciting incident that disrupts the routine and creates a problem.

- **Because of that:** Detail the actions taken to address the problem.

- **Until finally:** Describe the resolution and the positive outcome.

- **And ever since:** Highlight lasting impact and transformation.

For example, if you're presenting a new e-commerce platform, your story might go like this:

- Once upon a time, a small business owner named Alex struggled to reach customers online.

- Every day, Alex spent hours managing inventory and trying to boost online sales with little success.

- One day, Alex discovered your e-commerce platform.

- Because of that, Alex could easily set up an online store, manage inventory, and reach a wider audience.

- Finally, Alex's business started to thrive, with increased sales and customer engagement.

- And since then, Alex has enjoyed the benefits of a successful online presence, thanks to your platform.

## Storytelling in Your Portfolio

Your design portfolio is your professional storybook. It should showcase your skills and projects and the narratives behind your work. Here's how you can infuse storytelling into your portfolio:

**Project Case Studies:** Provide a detailed case study that follows a storytelling structure for each project. Describe the problem, your design process, your challenges, and the results you achieved. Use visuals, such as sketches, wireframes, motion graphics and prototypes, to enhance your narrative.

**User Stories:** Include user stories to highlight the impact of your designs on real people. Describe specific scenarios where your design made a difference in the user's life. Use quotes, testimonials, and anecdotes to add authenticity and emotional depth.

**Process Narratives:** Share the journey of your design process, from initial research to final implementation. Describe the methods and tools you used, your decisions, and the iterations you went through. Highlight key moments of insight and learning.

**Visual Storytelling:** Use visuals strategically to support your narrative. Incorporate before-and-after comparisons, journey maps, empathy maps, and user flows to illustrate your design process and outcomes. Visuals can make your story more engaging and easier to understand.

**Reflective Insights:** End each case study with reflective insights. Discuss what you learned from the project, how it influenced your design thinking, and what you would do differently in the future. This reflection adds depth to your narrative and shows your growth as a designer.

## Personal Narratives: Sharing Your Journey

In addition to project-based storytelling, your portfolio should also tell the story of your journey as a designer. This narrative helps potential employers and clients understand who you are, what drives you, and what makes you unique. Here are some tips for crafting your personal narrative:

**Origin Story:** Share how you became interested in design. Describe the moments, experiences, or influences that sparked your passion. This origin story provides context for your journey and helps your audience connect with you personally.

**Career Milestones:** Highlight critical milestones in your career, such as significant projects, collaborations, or achievements. Describe the challenges you faced and the lessons you learned along the way. These milestones illustrate your growth and development as a designer.

**Design Philosophy:** Articulate your design philosophy and principles. Explain what drives your design decisions, what values you prioritise, and what goals you aim to achieve through your work. This philosophy gives insight into your approach and mindset.

**Future Aspirations:** Share your future aspirations and goals. Describe what you hope to achieve in your career, the impact you want to make, and the areas you want to explore. This forward-looking narrative demonstrates your ambition and vision.

## Crafting Stories for Presentations

Presentations are another powerful medium for storytelling. Whether you're presenting to clients, stakeholders, or peers, a well-crafted narrative can make your message more persuasive and memorable. Here are some tips for incorporating storytelling into your presentations:

**Start with a Hook:** Begin your presentation with a compelling hook that grabs your audience's attention. This could be a surprising statistic, a provocative question, or a relatable anecdote. The hook sets the stage for your narrative and piques interest.

**Build a Narrative Arc:** Structure your presentation with a clear narrative arc. Introduce the context and problem, detail your design process and solutions, and conclude with the results and impact. This arc guides your audience through a cohesive story.

**Use Visuals Effectively:** Use visuals to support and enhance your narrative. Incorporate images, diagrams, and videos to illustrate key points and make your story more engaging. Avoid cluttered slides and focus on visuals that add value to your narrative.

**Engage Emotionally:** Connect with your audience emotionally by sharing personal stories, user testimonials, and impactful anecdotes. Emotions make your narrative more memorable and persuasive.

**Reinforce Key Messages:** Throughout your presentation, reinforce key messages and takeaways. Use repetition, summaries, and calls to action to ensure your audience retains the most critical points.

## Storytelling to Sell

In design, storytelling is not just a tool for communication; it's a powerful strategy for selling your ideas, products, and services. Whether you're pitching a concept to a client, presenting a design to stakeholders, or marketing a product to consumers, a well-crafted story can make all the difference.

### Pitching to Clients

When pitching to clients, storytelling helps you connect with them on a deeper level and make your proposal more compelling. Instead of simply presenting features and specifications, tell a story that illustrates the value and impact of your design.

For example, suppose you're pitching a new branding concept for a company. In that case, you might start by telling the story of "Emily," a potential customer who feels confused and disconnected from the brand. Describe how your new branding will create a cohesive and engaging experience for Emily, making her feel understood and valued. This narrative highlights the benefits of your design and makes it relatable and emotionally resonant.

## Presenting to Stakeholders

Storytelling can help you build a persuasive case for your design decisions when presenting to stakeholders. Use stories to illustrate the problem, the design process, and the outcomes, making your presentation more engaging and convincing.

For instance, if you're presenting a redesign of a product's user interface, you might tell the story of "Mark," a user who struggles with the current interface. Describe Mark's frustrations and how your redesign addresses these pain points, resulting in a more intuitive and satisfying user experience. This narrative helps stakeholders understand your design's rationale and its potential impact.

## Marketing to Consumers

In marketing and advertising, storytelling is a powerful way to connect with consumers and build brand loyalty. By telling stories that resonate with your target audience, you can create a strong emotional connection and differentiate your brand from competitors.

Consider the example of a sustainable fashion brand. Instead of simply promoting eco-friendly materials and ethical manufacturing practices, the brand tells the story of "Lily," a conscious consumer who wants to make a positive impact through her choices. The brand shares Lily's journey of discovering their products, her satisfaction with their quality and style, and her pride in supporting a sustainable brand. This story highlights the brand's values and inspires and motivates consumers to join the movement.

## Branding and Storytelling

Brands are built on stories. The most successful brands tell compelling stories that resonate with their audience, create a strong emotional connection, and communicate their values and vision. Here are some ways to use storytelling in branding:

### Brand Story

Your brand story is the narrative that encapsulates your brand's identity, mission, and values. It should convey who you are, what you stand for, and why you exist. A powerful brand story can differentiate you from competitors, build trust, and foster loyalty.

For example, TOMS's brand story revolves around the mission of providing shoes to children in need. The "One for One" story—where TOMS donates a pair of shoes to a child in need for every pair of shoes purchased— resonates deeply with consumers and creates a strong emotional connection. This narrative communicates the brand's values and inspires and engages the audience.

### Product Stories

Every product has a story. Telling the story of how a product was created, the problem it solves, and its impact on users can make it more relatable and compelling.

For instance, Apple excels at telling product stories. When launching a new product, Apple doesn't just highlight the features; it tells the story of how the product was designed to enhance users' lives. They share the innovation journey, meticulous attention to detail, and the user experiences that inspired the design. These stories create anticipation, excitement, and a solid emotional connection with the audience.

## Customer Stories

Customer stories are powerful testimonials that highlight the real-life impact of your products or services. By sharing your customers' experiences and successes, you can build credibility, trust, and loyalty.

For example, Airbnb often shares stories of hosts and guests, showcasing the unique and meaningful experiences facilitated by their platform. These stories humanise the brand, build trust, and inspire others to join the community. They illustrate the brand's mission of creating a world where anyone can belong anywhere.

## Visual Storytelling

Visual storytelling is a powerful way to enhance your narrative and make it more engaging and memorable. Here are some techniques for incorporating visual storytelling into your design work:

## Visual Metaphors

Use visual metaphors to convey complex ideas and emotions in a simple and relatable way. Visual metaphors can make abstract concepts more tangible and memorable.

For example, a campaign promoting financial literacy might use the metaphor of a tree growing from a tiny seed, symbolising the growth and potential of wise financial decisions. This visual metaphor makes the concept of financial literacy more accessible and impactful.

## Data Visualization

Data visualisation transforms raw data into compelling visual stories. Charts, graphs, and infographics can make data more understandable and engaging.

For instance, a health organisation might use data visualisation to tell the story of a public health initiative. They could create an infographic that illustrates the initiative's impact on community health, using visuals to highlight key statistics and outcomes. This approach makes the data more relatable and persuasive.

## Interactive Storytelling

Interactive storytelling engages your audience by allowing them to participate in the narrative. This can be achieved through interactive websites, apps, or multimedia experiences.

For example, a travel company might create an interactive website that allows users to explore different travel destinations through immersive stories and virtual tours. Users can navigate through the narrative, discover hidden gems, and create their own travel itinerary. This interactive experience makes the storytelling more engaging and memorable.

## The Impact of Storytelling on Product Design

Storytelling isn't just a tool for communication and marketing; it's also a powerful strategy for product design. By integrating storytelling into the design process, you can create products that resonate deeply with users and stand out in the market.

### User-Centred Design

Storytelling helps you adopt a user-centred approach to design. By understanding and telling your users' stories, you can create products that address their needs, solve their problems, and enhance their lives.

For example, a team designing a new kitchen appliance might start by telling the story of "Mira," a busy mother who struggles to prepare healthy meals for her family. By focusing on Mira's needs and challenges, the team can design an appliance that makes cooking easier, faster, and more enjoyable. This user-centred approach ensures that the product resonates with its target audience and meets their real needs.

## Emotional Design

Storytelling adds an emotional dimension to design. By telling stories that evoke emotions, you can create products that connect with users on a deeper level and inspire loyalty.

Consider the fitness tracker example. Instead of just promoting the technical features, the brand tells the story of "Tom," who used the tracker to train for his first marathon. The story highlights Tom's journey, his challenges, and his sense of accomplishment when he crosses the finish line. This emotional narrative makes the product more relatable and inspiring, encouraging other users to embark on their own fitness journeys.

## Differentiation

In a crowded market, storytelling helps you differentiate your product from competitors. By telling a unique and compelling story, you can create a distinctive brand identity and stand out in the minds of consumers.

For instance, the story of the first pair of Levi's jeans, designed for gold miners during the California Gold Rush, sets the brand apart as a symbol of rugged durability and American heritage. This narrative differentiates Levi's from other denim brands and creates a solid emotional connection with consumers.

## Conclusion: The Art and Power of Storytelling

Crafting compelling narratives is an essential skill for designers. It allows us to communicate our ideas, engage our audience, and drive meaningful change. By incorporating storytelling into our work and portfolio, we can elevate our message and create a lasting impact.

Remember, a compelling story is more than just a sequence of events. It's about connecting with your audience emotionally, making abstract concepts tangible, and highlighting the human experience. Whether you're presenting a design concept, sharing user research, or showcasing your work, storytelling can transform your narrative and make it resonate deeply with your audience.

So, embrace the art of storytelling. Use it to illuminate your ideas, amplify your message, and inspire action. Let your stories bridge you to your audience, and let them see the world through your eyes. The power of storytelling is within you. Use it wisely, and watch your designs come to life in ways you never imagined.

# CHAPTER 3

## Mastering the Timeless Fundamentals

In the ever-evolving design landscape, tools and technologies may change, but the fundamentals remain constant. These timeless principles form the bedrock of our craft, guiding us to create work that is not only functional but also beautiful, meaningful, and impactful. Mastering these fundamentals is akin to learning the scales in music or the basic steps in dance; they provide the foundation for creativity to flourish. This chapter delves into the core principles of design, offering practical advice and frameworks to help you master these essentials and elevate your work.

### The Importance of Fundamentals in Design

The fundamentals of design are the principles and elements that underpin all successful creative work. They include concepts such as balance, contrast, hierarchy, alignment, proximity, repetition, and space. These principles are not arbitrary rules but are grounded in human psychology and perception, helping us create aesthetically pleasing and easily understood designs.

Understanding and mastering these fundamentals enables designers to create work that communicates effectively, resonates with audiences, and stands the test of time. Whether you're designing a logo, a website, a product, or an experience, these principles will guide your decisions and enhance your creative process.

## Core Design Principles

Let's explore some of the key principles of design in greater detail, along with practical examples and advice on how to apply them in your work.

### Balance

Balance refers to the distribution of visual weight within a design. It can be symmetrical (evenly distributed) or asymmetrical (uneven but still balanced). Achieving balance ensures that a design feels stable and visually pleasing.

**Practical Advice:**

- **Symmetrical Balance:** Use symmetrical balance for formal, traditional, or orderly designs—for example, a website layout with centred navigation and evenly spaced elements.

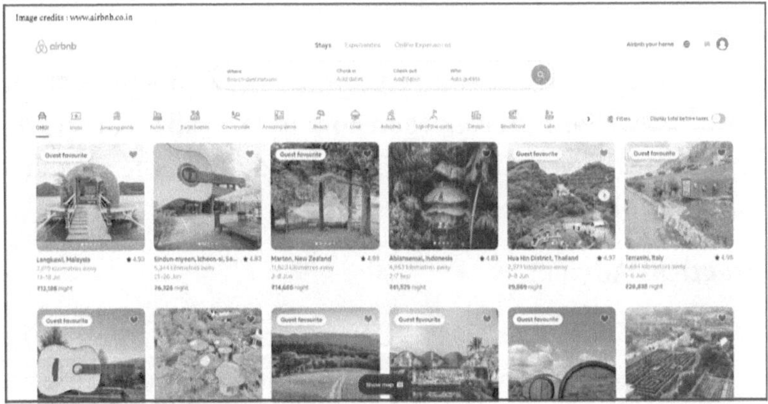

- **Asymmetrical Balance:** Use asymmetrical balance for dynamic, modern, or creative designs. For instance, a magazine cover with a large image on one side and text on the other, balanced by contrasting colours and shapes.

**Example:** Consider the iconic Apple logo. The logo is asymmetrical but balanced, with the bite on the right side providing visual interest without making the design feel off-kilter. This balance contributes to its timeless appeal.

## Contrast

Contrast creates visual interest and highlights important elements using differences in colour, size, shape, texture, or type. It helps to draw attention and guide the viewer's eye through the design.

**Practical Advice:**

- **Colour Contrast:** Use contrasting colours to make key elements stand out—for example, a call-to-action button in a bright colour against a muted background.

- **Size Contrast:** Vary the size of elements to create a hierarchy. For instance, a larger headline followed by smaller body text to indicate importance.

**Example:** Nike's branding employs high contrast in its advertisements, often using black-and-white imagery with a bold, bright-coloured swoosh. This contrast makes the logo instantly recognisable and emphasises the brand's dynamic and energetic identity.

## Hierarchy

Hierarchy is the arrangement of elements to indicate their order of importance. It guides the viewer's eye to the most crucial information first, then to secondary details.

**Practical Advice:**

- **Typographic Hierarchy:** Use different font sizes, weights, and styles to create a clear hierarchy. For example, a headline should be in bold, large type, subheadings in medium type, and body text in regular, smaller type.

- **Visual Hierarchy:** Arrange elements based on their importance. Place the most critical information at the top or centre of the design.

**Example:** In news websites like The New York Times, visual and typographic hierarchies are used to prioritise information. Headlines are large and bold, subheadings are smaller, and body text is the smallest. Images and key stories are prominently placed to catch the reader's attention first.

## Alignment

Alignment ensures that elements are visually connected and arranged coherently. Proper alignment creates order and organisation within a design.

**Practical Advice:**

- **Grid Systems:** Use grid systems to align elements consistently. Grids help maintain order and proportionality.

- **Edge Alignment:** Align text and elements along edges (left, right, centre) to create a structured layout.

**Example:** The Google homepage is a classic example of alignment. The search bar and buttons are perfectly centred, providing a clean, organised appearance that is easy to use and visually appealing.

## Proximity

Proximity groups related elements together, reducing clutter and improving readability. Elements that are close together are perceived as related, while those that are far apart are seen as separate.

**Practical Advice:**

- **Grouping:** Group related elements together, such as contact information, navigation links, or product details.

- **Whitespace:** Use whitespace strategically to separate unrelated elements and prevent overcrowding.

**Example:** In print design, business cards often use proximity to group information. The person's name, title, and contact information are grouped together, separated by whitespace from the company logo and other details.

## Repetition

Repetition creates consistency and cohesion in a design. Repeating elements such as colours, shapes, fonts, and textures reinforces the overall look and feel.

**Practical Advice:**

- **Consistent Styling:** Use consistent styling for headers, subheaders, and body text across different pages or sections.

- **Pattern Repetition:** Repeat design patterns, such as icons or decorative elements, to create a unified theme.

**Example:** In branding, Coca-Cola effectively uses repetition. The iconic red colour, cursive logo, and ribbon design are repeated across all marketing materials, creating a solid and cohesive brand identity.

## Space

Space, or whitespace, refers to the empty areas around and between elements. It provides breathing room, improves readability, and enhances the overall aesthetic of a design.

**Practical Advice:**

- **Margins and Padding:** Use adequate margins and padding around elements to create a balanced layout.

- **Whitespace as a Design Element:** Treat whitespace as an active element in your design, not just an absence of content.

**Example:** Apple's product pages use generous whitespace to highlight their sleek design. The ample space around images and text draws attention to the products and enhances the brand's premium feel.

## Frameworks for Mastering Design Fundamentals

Adopting structured frameworks and methodologies is essential for mastering the timeless fundamentals of design. These frameworks provide a systematic approach to learning, practising, and applying design principles.

## The Design Thinking Framework

Design Thinking is a human-centred approach to problem-solving that emphasises empathy, creativity, and iteration. It consists of five stages: empathise, Define, Ideate, Prototype, and Test. This framework helps designers create innovative and user-centred solutions.

### Design Thinking Framework

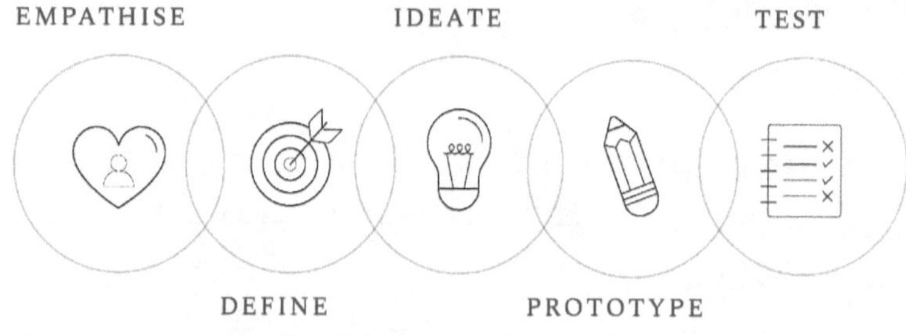


**Empathise:** Understand users' needs through observation, interviews, and research.

**Define:** Clearly articulate the problem you're trying to solve based on insights from the Empathise stage.

**Ideate:** Generate a wide range of ideas and solutions through brainstorming and creative thinking.

**Prototype:** Create low-fidelity prototypes to explore different solutions and gather feedback.

**Test:** Test the prototypes with users, gather feedback, and refine the solutions.

**Example:** IDEO, a global design and innovation company, uses the Design Thinking framework to tackle complex problems. For instance, when designing a new shopping cart, IDEO's team followed the Design Thinking process to understand users' needs, generate innovative ideas, and create a functional and user-friendly cart.

## IDEO - Design Thinking framework

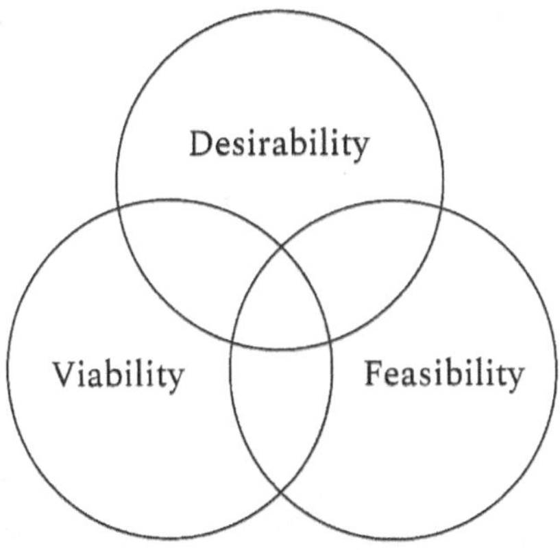


**The Double Diamond Model**

The Double Diamond Model, developed by the Design Council, visually represents the design process. It consists of four phases: Discover, Define, Develop, and Deliver. This model emphasises the divergent and convergent thinking stages in design.

**Divergent Thinking:** Divergent thinking involves generating a wide range of ideas and solutions without immediate judgement or criticism. It's about exploring many possibilities and thinking broadly.

**Convergent Thinking:** Convergent thinking involves narrowing down the options generated during the divergent phase to select the most viable and effective solution. It's about critical evaluation and decision-making.

# Double Diamond Model

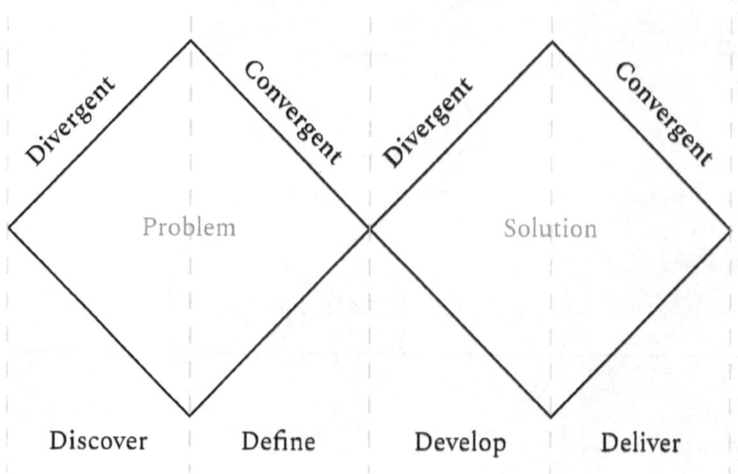


**Discover:** Gather insights and explore the problem space broadly.

**Define:** Narrow down and define the core problem or opportunity.

**Develop:** Generate and develop potential solutions through iteration and refinement.

**Deliver:** Finalise and implement the solution, ensuring it meets user needs and goals.

**Example:** The Double Diamond Model was used to redesign the UK's GOV website. The design team conducted extensive user research during the Discover phase, defined the core problems in the Define phase, developed prototypes and solutions in the Develop phase, and delivered a streamlined, user-friendly government website in the Deliver phase.

## Practical Steps for Mastering Fundamentals

**Study and Observe:** Analyse successful designs in various fields, such as graphic design, architecture, product design, and web design. Observe how the fundamentals are applied and learn from real-world examples.

**Practice and Experiment:** Regular practice is essential for mastering design fundamentals. Experiment with different layouts, colour schemes, and typographic treatments. Use design challenges and personal projects to hone your skills.

**Seek Feedback:** Share your work with peers, mentors, and users to gather constructive feedback. Use this feedback to identify areas for improvement and refine your designs.

**Learn Continuously:** Stay updated with the latest design trends, tools, and techniques. Attend workshops, read design books, and follow industry blogs to sharpen your skills.

**Reflect and Iterate:** Reflect on your design process and outcomes. Identify what worked well and what could be improved. Use this reflection to iterate and enhance your future designs.

## Real-World Applications of Design Fundamentals

To illustrate the application of design fundamentals, let's explore some real-world examples:

### Web Design: Airbnb

Airbnb's website is a prime example of mastering design fundamentals. The site uses a clean, grid-based layout (alignment) with ample whitespace (space) to create a balanced and visually appealing design. High-quality images (contrast) draw attention to the properties, while the clear typographic hierarchy (hierarchy) guides users through the content. Consistent styling and repeated elements (repetition) create a cohesive and professional look.

### Product Design: Dyson

Dyson's vacuum cleaners exemplify the application of design fundamentals in product design. The products are designed with a focus on balance and ergonomics (balance), making them easy to use and handle. Using contrasting colours and materials (contrast) highlights key features and functionalities. Dyson's design process involves extensive user research and testing (empathy and iteration), ensuring that the products meet users' needs and provide a superior experience.

## Branding: Coca-Cola

Coca-Cola's branding is a masterclass in using design fundamentals. The brand's iconic red and white colour scheme (contrast) is instantly recognisable and creates a strong visual impact. Using consistent typography and logo placement (repetition) reinforces brand identity across all marketing materials. The brand's storytelling (emotional design) connects with consumers on a deeper level, creating a loyal and engaged customer base.

## When to Break the Rules

While mastering the fundamentals is crucial, knowing when and how to break these rules can lead to innovative and impactful designs. The fundamentals provide a strong foundation, but they should not constrain creativity. Understanding the principles deeply allows you to make informed decisions about when to deviate from them for a greater purpose.

## Context and Audience

The context and audience of your design often dictate when it's appropriate to break the rules. For example, a children's book might benefit from asymmetrical balance and vibrant, clashing colours to capture attention and convey a sense of fun and excitement. In contrast, a corporate financial report would likely adhere more strictly to traditional design principles to convey professionalism and reliability.

**Example:** The website for the Museum of Modern Art (MoMA) breaks several design conventions to create a unique and engaging user experience. The use of unconventional layouts, bold typography, and unexpected interactions aligns with the museum's avant-garde identity and appeals to its audience of art enthusiasts and creatives.

## Innovation and Creativity

Pushing the boundaries of traditional design principles can lead to groundbreaking innovations. When designing a new product or experience, experimenting with the fundamentals can result in fresh, unexpected solutions.

**Example:** Google's Material Design introduced a new design language that broke away from the skeuomorphic design trends of the past. By emphasising bold colours, grid-based layouts, and responsive animations, Material Design created a more intuitive and engaging user experience that has since influenced design standards across the industry.

## Expressing Brand Identity

Breaking design rules can help express a brand's unique identity and differentiate it from competitors. Brands that aim to be seen as innovative, rebellious, or unconventional might deliberately break traditional design rules to communicate these values.

**Example:** Red Bull's branding is a prime example of using design to express a unique identity. The brand's energetic and adventurous image is conveyed through dynamic layouts, vibrant colours, and bold typography, often breaking traditional design rules to stand out and capture the spirit of its target audience.

## Conclusion: The Timelessness of Design Fundamentals

Mastering the timeless fundamentals of design is essential for creating functional, aesthetically pleasing, and impactful work. These principles provide the foundation for all creative endeavours, guiding us to make informed design decisions and solve problems effectively. However, truly mastering these fundamentals includes knowing when and how to break them to achieve greater creative heights.

By understanding and applying the core principles of balance, contrast, hierarchy, alignment, proximity, repetition, and space, you can elevate your design work and create experiences that resonate with users. Embrace structured frameworks such as Design Thinking and the Double Diamond Model to approach design challenges systematically and creatively.

Continuously study, practice, seek feedback, and reflect on your work. By doing so, you'll develop a deep understanding of these principles and the ability to apply them intuitively and effectively. And when the situation calls for it, don't be afraid to break the rules and push the boundaries of traditional design.

# CHAPTER 4

## Curiosity Unleashed

Curiosity is the spark that ignites creativity and fuels innovation. It drives us to explore, question, and seek new understanding. For designers, curiosity is not just a trait but a fundamental necessity. It leads us to discover fresh perspectives, uncover hidden insights, and develop groundbreaking solutions. This chapter delves into the essence of curiosity, offering practical advice and frameworks to help you cultivate a growth mindset and embrace continuous learning. Get ready to unleash your curiosity and elevate your creative potential.

### The Power of Curiosity

Curiosity is the engine of exploration. It propels us to venture beyond the familiar and delve into the unknown. It challenges our assumptions, broadens our horizons, and enriches our understanding. In the context of design, curiosity inspires us to:

**Seek New Insights:** By asking questions and exploring different perspectives, we gain deeper insights into user needs, behaviours, and motivations.

**Foster Innovation:** Curiosity leads us to experiment with new ideas, techniques, and technologies, driving innovation and creativity.

**Enhance Empathy:** By being curious about others' experiences and viewpoints, we develop greater empathy and create user-centred designs.

**Adapt and Grow:** Curiosity keeps us open to learning and adapting, ensuring that we stay relevant and effective in a constantly changing landscape.

## The Life-Enriching Benefits of Curiosity

Curiosity isn't just beneficial for professional growth; it profoundly impacts personal development and life satisfaction. Embracing curiosity can lead to:

**Increased Knowledge and Skills:** By continuously seeking new information, you expand your knowledge base and develop a diverse skill set.

**Improved Problem-Solving:** Curiosity drives you to explore multiple solutions and think creatively, enhancing your problem-solving abilities.

**Greater Adaptability:** Curiosity makes you more open to change and new experiences, fostering adaptability in personal and professional contexts.

**Enhanced Relationships:** Being curious about others' perspectives and experiences deepens your connections and improves your interpersonal relationships.

**Lifelong Fulfilment:** A curious mindset leads to a more engaging and fulfilling life filled with continuous learning and personal growth.

## Practical Advice for Cultivating Curiosity

Curiosity is a skill that can be nurtured and developed. Here are some practical steps to help you cultivate a curious mindset:

**Ask Questions:** Cultivate the habit of asking open-ended questions. Instead of accepting things at face value, ask "why," "how," and "what if." Questions stimulate thinking and lead to deeper understanding.

**Embrace Lifelong Learning:** Commit to continuous learning. Read books, attend workshops, take online courses, and stay updated with industry trends. The more you learn, the more curious you'll become.

**Explore Diverse Interests:** Diversify your interests and explore fields outside of your primary domain. Cross-disciplinary knowledge can inspire new ideas and approaches in your design work.

**Engage in Active Observation:** Observe the world around you with a keen eye. Pay attention to details, notice patterns, and analyse behaviours. Observation sharpens your ability to see beyond the obvious.

**Experiment and Play:** Allow yourself to experiment and play with ideas. Try new tools, techniques, and methods without the fear of failure. Playfulness stimulates creativity and encourages curiosity.

**Reflect and Journal:** Take time to reflect on your experiences and insights. Keep a journal to document your thoughts, ideas, and questions. Reflection helps you make connections and deepen your understanding.

## Frameworks for Cultivating a Growth Mindset

As defined by psychologist Carol Dweck, a growth mindset is the belief that abilities and intelligence can be developed through dedication and hard work. This mindset is essential for fostering curiosity and embracing continuous learning. Here are some frameworks to help you cultivate a growth mindset:

### Learning Zone Framework

The Learning Zone Framework is a model that illustrates how individuals can optimise their learning and growth by navigating through three distinct zones: the Comfort Zone, the Learning Zone, and the Panic Zone. This framework helps people understand where they need to be to maximise learning and development while avoiding burnout or stagnation.

### Comfort Zone

- **Characteristics:** The Comfort Zone is where individuals feel safe and in control. They perform tasks and activities they are familiar with, which leads to minimal stress and little growth.

- **Impact on Learning:** Spending too much time in the Comfort Zone can lead to complacency and a lack of progress. While it's essential for maintaining confidence and stability, it doesn't offer significant opportunities for new learning.

## Learning Zone

- **Characteristics:** The Learning Zone is where individuals stretch beyond their comfort level but not so far that they become overwhelmed. Here, they encounter challenges and new experiences that require them to develop new skills and knowledge.

- **Impact on Learning:** This is the optimal zone for growth and development. Individuals are engaged, motivated, and capable of absorbing new information. Constructive feedback and support from mentors or peers can be particularly beneficial in this zone.

## Panic Zone

- **Characteristics:** The Panic Zone is where individuals feel overwhelmed and stressed. Tasks and challenges here are too complex, leading to anxiety, fear, and a potential shutdown of learning processes.

- **Impact on Learning:** Operating in the Panic Zone can be detrimental. High-stress levels can impede the ability to learn and retain information, and prolonged exposure can lead to burnout.

**Example:** Imagine a graphic designer who is very comfortable with traditional print media (Comfort Zone). To grow, they decide to learn UX design (Learning Zone). They start by taking an online course and working on a small web project. Throughout this process, they seek feedback from their colleagues and join a community of UX designers. Suppose they were to jump directly into a highly complex project without any prior knowledge or support. In that case, they might end up in the Panic Zone, feeling overwhelmed and unable to progress.

By understanding and applying the Learning Zone Framework, individuals can strategically manage their learning experiences to foster continuous growth and avoid the pitfalls of stagnation or burnout.

## The Feedback Loop Framework

The Feedback Loop Framework emphasises the importance of seeking and incorporating feedback to facilitate growth and improvement. It involves four stages: Action, Feedback, Reflection, and Adjustment.

- **Action:** Take action and execute tasks based on your current knowledge and skills.

- **Feedback:** Seek feedback from peers, mentors, and users. Feedback provides valuable insights into your performance and areas for improvement.

- **Reflection:** Reflect on the feedback received. Analyse the information, identify patterns, and draw meaningful conclusions.

- **Adjustment:** Adjust your approach based on the reflection. Implement changes, experiment with new strategies, and iterate on your work.

**Example:** A UX designer might create a prototype for a new app feature and test it with users. The feedback received highlights usability issues and areas for enhancement. Reflecting on this feedback, the designer identifies specific improvements and adjusts the design accordingly. This iterative process ensures the end product meets user needs and expectations.

## Different Approaches to Learning

Embracing diverse learning approaches can enhance your curiosity and drive continuous growth. Here are some effective learning methods for designers:

### Self-Directed Learning

Self-directed learning involves taking initiative and responsibility for your learning journey. It empowers you to explore topics of interest, set learning goals, and pursue knowledge at your own pace.

**Practical Steps:**

- **Identify Learning Goals:** Define clear and achievable learning goals based on your interests and career aspirations.

- **Curate Resources:** Gather various learning resources, such as books, online courses, podcasts, and articles, that align with your goals.

- **Create a Learning Plan:** Develop a structured learning plan that outlines the steps and timeline for achieving your goals.

- **Track Progress:** Monitor your progress regularly and adjust your plan as needed. Celebrate milestones and reflect on your achievements.

**Example:** A designer interested in mastering motion graphics might set a learning goal to become proficient in Adobe After Effects. They curate resources, such as tutorials, courses, and design blogs, and create a learning plan to practise specific techniques and complete projects over six months. Tracking their progress and seeking feedback, they steadily improve their skills and achieve their goal.

## Collaborative Learning

Collaborative learning involves learning from and with others. It fosters knowledge sharing, diverse perspectives, and collective problem-solving.

**Practical Steps:**

- **Join Learning Communities:** Connect with fellow designers by participating in design communities, forums, and social media groups.

- **Seek Mentorship:** Find mentors who can provide guidance, share insights, and offer feedback on your work.

- **Collaborate on Projects:** Work on collaborative projects with peers in a professional setting or through design challenges and hackathons.

- **Engage in Peer Reviews:** Regularly review and critique each other's work to provide constructive feedback and learn from different viewpoints.

**Example:** A group of UX designers might form a study group to explore advanced user research techniques. They meet weekly to discuss research articles, share experiences, and collaborate on a mock project. Through peer reviews and discussions, they deepen their understanding and apply new methods to their work.

## Experiential Learning

Experiential learning emphasises learning through hands-on experience and real-world application. It involves actively engaging in projects, experiments, and activities that provide practical insights and skills.

**Practical Steps:**

- **Engage in Real-World Projects:** Seek opportunities to work on real-world design projects, whether through internships, freelance work, or volunteer initiatives.

- **Participate in Workshops:** Attend workshops and hands-on training sessions that offer practical experience and skill-building.

- **Experiment and Iterate:** Embrace a mindset of experimentation. Try new techniques, tools, and approaches, and iterate based on the outcomes.

- **Reflect on Experiences:** After completing a project or experiment, reflect on the experience. Identify what you learned, what worked well, and what could be improved.

**Example:** A graphic designer might volunteer to design promotional materials for a local nonprofit organisation. Through this real-world project, they gain hands-on experience, experiment with different design styles, and receive feedback from the organisation. Reflecting on the experience, the designer identifies critical takeaways and areas for further improvement.

## Curiosity and Personal Growth

Curiosity extends beyond professional development; it plays a crucial role in personal growth and fulfilment. Here are some ways curiosity can enrich your life:

### Expanding Horizons

Curiosity encourages you to explore new topics, cultures, and experiences. Expanding your horizons gives you a broader perspective and a deeper understanding of different viewpoints.

**Practical Steps:**

- **Travel and Explore:** Travel to new places and immerse yourself in different cultures. Experience new foods, traditions and lifestyles.

- **Read Widely:** Read books, articles and blogs on various subjects. Explore genres and topics outside your usual interests.

- **Attend Events:** Participate in conferences, workshops, and cultural events. Engage with people from diverse backgrounds and industries.

**Example:** Travelling to a foreign country and experiencing its culture firsthand can profoundly impact your worldview. It can inspire new ideas, enhance your empathy, and provide fresh perspectives to apply to your personal and professional life.

## Building Meaningful Relationships

Curiosity about others fosters deeper and more meaningful relationships. Genuine interest in people's stories, experiences, and perspectives can build stronger connections and enhance social interactions.

**Practical Steps:**

- **Ask Thoughtful Questions:** When interacting with others, ask open-ended questions, encouraging them to share their experiences and viewpoints.

- **Listen Actively:** Practise active listening by paying full attention to the speaker, acknowledging their points, and responding thoughtfully.

- **Show Empathy:** Show genuine empathy and understanding. Validate their feelings and experiences, and offer support and encouragement.

**Example:** In a professional setting, being curious about your colleagues' backgrounds and experiences can lead to stronger teamwork and collaboration. Understanding their motivations and perspectives can enhance communication and foster a positive work environment.

## Enhancing Problem-Solving Skills

Curiosity drives you to explore multiple solutions and think creatively, enhancing your problem-solving abilities. It encourages you to approach challenges with an open mind and a willingness to experiment.

**Practical Steps:**

- **Embrace Challenges:** View challenges as opportunities for growth and learning. Approach problems with curiosity and a solution-oriented mindset.

- **Brainstorm Solutions:** Engage in brainstorming sessions to generate a wide range of potential solutions. Consider unconventional and innovative approaches.

- **Experiment and Iterate:** Test different solutions and iterate based on the results. Be open to learning from failures and refining your approach.

**Example:** When faced with a complex design problem, a curious mindset can lead to creative and effective solutions. You can overcome challenges and achieve better outcomes by exploring various approaches, seeking feedback, and iterating on your designs.

## Curiosity and the Creative Process

Curiosity plays a pivotal role in the creative process. It drives designers to explore new possibilities, push boundaries, and discover innovative solutions. Here are some ways to integrate curiosity into your creative process:

### Research and Exploration

Curiosity fuels the research and exploration phase of the creative process. By seeking diverse sources of inspiration and conducting thorough research, designers can uncover new ideas and insights.

### Practical Steps:

- **Explore Diverse Sources:** Seek inspiration from various fields, such as art, science, nature, and culture. Explore design blogs, museums, and exhibitions to gather diverse perspectives.

- **Conduct User Research:** Conduct user research to understand your target audience's needs, behaviours, and preferences. Use techniques like interviews, surveys, and ethnographic studies.

- **Analyse Trends:** Stay updated with industry trends and emerging technologies. Analyse how these trends can be integrated into your design work.

**Example:** When tasked with designing a new wearable device, a product designer might explore diverse sources of inspiration, such as fashion design, biomimicry, and emerging tech trends. They conduct user research to understand the needs of potential users and analyse how current market trends can influence their design. This comprehensive exploration leads to a unique and innovative product concept.

## Ideation and Brainstorming

Curiosity drives the ideation and brainstorming phase, encouraging designers to generate a wide range of ideas and explore unconventional solutions.

**Practical Steps:**

- **Divergent Thinking:** Encourage divergent thinking by generating as many ideas as possible without judgement. Use techniques such as mind mapping, sketching, and brainstorming sessions.

- **Embrace Unconventional Ideas:** Be open to unconventional and "out-of-the-box" ideas. Allow yourself to explore wild and imaginative concepts.

- **Collaborative Ideation:** Engage in collaborative ideation sessions with diverse team members. Different perspectives can lead to richer and more innovative ideas.

**Example:** A design team working on a new social media app might conduct a brainstorming session using mind mapping. They encourage all team members to contribute ideas, no matter how unconventional. This collaborative ideation leads to the development of unique features that set the app apart from competitors.

## Prototyping and Testing

Curiosity is essential during the prototyping and testing phase, driving designers to experiment, iterate, and refine their solutions.

**Practical Steps:**

- **Create Low-Fidelity Prototypes:** Start with low-fidelity prototypes to quickly test and explore different ideas. Use sketches, wireframes, and basic models.

- **Conduct User Testing:** Test prototypes with real users to gather feedback and insights. Observe how users interact with the design and identify areas for improvement.

- **Iterate and Refine:** Use the feedback from user testing to iterate and refine the design. Embrace a mindset of continuous improvement.

**Example:** A UX designer designing a new website feature might create low-fidelity wireframes and test them with users. Based on the feedback, they iterate on the design, making adjustments to improve usability and user satisfaction. This iterative process ensures that the final design effectively meets user needs.

## Conclusion: The Boundless Potential of Curiosity

Curiosity is the driving force behind exploration, learning, and innovation. It empowers designers to seek new insights, foster creativity, and adapt to an ever-changing landscape. By cultivating a growth mindset, embracing diverse learning approaches, and integrating curiosity into the creative process, designers can unlock their full potential and create impactful, user-centred designs.

Curiosity isn't just a tool for professional development; it's a lifelong journey that enriches every aspect of our lives. It leads to continuous growth, deeper relationships, and a more fulfilling existence. Embrace curiosity with an open heart and an eager mind, and let it guide you to new discoveries and creative breakthroughs.

Remember, the journey of curiosity is ongoing. Continuously ask questions, seek new knowledge, and explore diverse perspectives. Embrace challenges and view them as opportunities for growth. Let curiosity be your guide, leading you to new discoveries and creative breakthroughs.

# CHAPTER 5

## Guiding Lights: Mentorship and Community

Mentorship and community are the guiding lights illuminating the path to growth and development. These relationships are invaluable in the design world, where innovation thrives on collaboration and shared knowledge. They provide support, inspiration, and learning opportunities that are crucial for both personal and professional growth. This chapter delves into the importance of mentorship and community, offering practical advice on finding the right mentors, building supportive networks, and leveraging these relationships to achieve your goals.

### The Role of Mentorship in Design

Mentorship is a powerful tool for growth. A good mentor can provide guidance, share valuable insights, and offer support through the challenges of a design career. They help you navigate complex projects, make informed career decisions, and avoid common pitfalls. Through regular interactions, mentors can help you develop and improve new skills. They provide constructive feedback, suggest learning resources, and share best practices. Mentors often have extensive professional networks and can introduce you to industry leaders, potential employers, and collaborative opportunities. A mentor's success stories can be powerful motivation, inspiring you to push your boundaries and strive for excellence.

Finding the right mentor involves identifying someone whose expertise aligns with your goals and who is genuinely interested in your growth. Clearly define what you want to achieve through mentorship—whether it's developing specific skills, advancing your career, or gaining insights into a particular industry. Look for professionals who have achieved what you aspire to. Attend industry events, join professional networks, and use platforms like LinkedIn and ADPList to find potential mentors. When approaching a potential mentor, be respectful and clear about your intentions. Explain why you admire their work and how they can help you achieve your goals. Show genuine interest in your mentor's work, be open to feedback, and demonstrate your commitment to growth.

Approaching a potential mentor can be daunting, but a structured framework can simplify the process and increase the likelihood of establishing a successful relationship.

# Finding the Right Mentor: A Structured Framework

## Self-Assessment:

- **Identify Your Needs:** Understand what specific areas you need help with. This could be technical skills, career advice, or industry insights.

- **Set Clear Goals:** Define what you want to achieve through mentorship. Clear goals will help you communicate your needs effectively.

## Research:

- **Identify Potential Mentors:** Look for individuals with expertise in your areas of interest. They could be industry leaders, experienced professionals, or academics.

- **Understand Their Work:** Study their work, follow their publications, and understand their career path. This will help you craft a personalised approach.

## Crafting the Approach:

- **Personalised Message:** Write a thoughtful and personalised message. Mention specific aspects of their work that inspire you and explain how their mentorship can help you achieve your goals.

- **Be Respectful and Professional:** Keep your message concise and professional. Acknowledge their time constraints and express your appreciation for their consideration.

**Building the Relationship:**

- **Regular Communication:** Establish a regular communication schedule. This could be bi-weekly or monthly meetings, depending on mutual availability.

- **Be Prepared:** Come to each session prepared with questions, discussion topics, and progress updates.

- **Show Gratitude:** Always express your gratitude for their time and insights. A mentor's guidance is a valuable gift.

**Giving Back:**

- **Share Your Learnings:** As you grow, share your knowledge and experiences with others. This could be through speaking at events, writing articles, or mentoring junior designers.

- **Contribute to the Community:** Actively participate in community events, forums, and discussions. Your contributions can help others grow and create a supportive environment for everyone.

## The Power of Community

Community is the collective force that propels us forward. It provides a sense of belonging, fosters collaboration, and creates a supportive environment for growth. Communities bring together individuals with diverse skills and experiences, fostering collaboration, idea exchange, and collective learning. Being part of a community provides emotional support and encouragement—a space where you can share your challenges, celebrate your successes, and find motivation. Communities often organise events, workshops, and networking opportunities, helping you gain exposure, learn new skills, and connect with industry leaders. Community members share resources such as design tools, learning materials, and job opportunities, enhancing your growth and productivity.

Building or joining a supportive community involves finding like-minded individuals who share your interests and goals. Determine what you are passionate about and what you want to gain from the community—be it learning new skills, networking, or finding collaborative opportunities. Look for existing communities that align with your interests, such as online forums, social media groups, or local meetups. Engage actively and contribute to discussions.

If you can't find a community that fits your needs, consider starting your own. Define the purpose, gather like-minded individuals, and create a welcoming and inclusive environment. Encourage active participation by organising events, discussions, and collaborative projects. Recognise contributions, celebrate achievements and support members.

To illustrate the power of community, consider the story of Designland, a community which I started with a bunch of friends to connect Indian designers from multiple backgrounds and unite them to grow better and learn from each other.

Designland has over 3000+ designers from India who work for top companies like Microsoft, Google, PhonePe, Razorpay, and many more. Through regular meetups, workshops, and online forums, it has become a vibrant hub for learning and collaboration.

Designland was initially intended to bring together people in one city, but it quickly expanded to multiple cities across India. Recognizing the potential for a larger, global community, I started "The Creativee Community" which is not only for designers but for all creative enthusiasts from diverse backgrounds. Members actively participate in discussions, share their work, and provide feedback to each other. We organise workshops where experienced creatives share their expertise on various topics such as art, music, theatre arts, and other creative fields. These sessions provide valuable learning opportunities and foster a sense of camaraderie and mutual support.

## Scaling Your Network

To maximise the benefits of mentorship and community, actively scale your network. Attend industry events like conferences, workshops and meetups. These events provide opportunities to meet industry professionals, learn from experts, and build relationships. Leverage online platforms like LinkedIn, Behance, and Dribbble to connect with professionals in your field. Engage with their content, join relevant groups, and initiate conversations. Participate in webinars and online courses to learn new skills and meet like-minded individuals. Collaborate on projects with peers in a professional setting or through design challenges and hackathons. Collaboration promotes deeper connections and mutual learning. Join professional associations such as AIGA (American Institute of Graphic Arts), IDSA (Industrial Designers Society of America), ADI (Association of Designers of India), The Creativee Community, which offer networking events, resources, and opportunities for professional development. Volunteer your time and expertise to community initiatives, nonprofit organisations, and educational programs. Giving back helps others, expands your network, and enhances your reputation.

## Networking with Authenticity

Networking isn't just about collecting business cards or adding contacts on LinkedIn. It's about forming genuine, mutually beneficial relationships. Approach networking with authenticity and a spirit of generosity. Show genuine interest in others' work and experiences. Offer help and support without expecting anything in return. Be a good listener, and engage in meaningful conversations. Authentic connections are built on trust and mutual respect, not on the expectation of immediate benefits. In a world where toxic networking can be prevalent, focus on creating a network based on genuine relationships and shared values. Avoid networking solely for personal gain. Instead, approach it with a mindset of mutual growth and collaboration. The relationships you build will be more meaningful and rewarding, leading to deeper connections and long-term support.

## Resources for Building and Engaging with Communities

To effectively build and engage with communities, utilise the right resources. Online communities and forums like Dribbble, Behance, and Reddit provide platforms for designers to showcase their work, get feedback, and connect with other creatives. Professional associations like AIGA, IDSA, and UXPA offer events, resources, and networking opportunities for designers. Networking platforms like LinkedIn, Meetup, and Eventbrite help you discover and attend industry events, workshops, and conferences. Learning platforms like Uxcel, Coursera, Skillshare, and Udemy offer online courses on design, technology, and business, providing opportunities for continuous learning and networking.

## The Impact of Mentorship and Community on Career Growth

Mentorship and community play a pivotal role in career growth. They provide a support system that helps you navigate the complexities of the design industry, build your skills, and achieve your goals. Regular interactions with mentors and community members help you stay updated with industry trends and continuously improve your skills. Networking within your community can open doors to new job opportunities, freelance projects, and collaborative ventures. Mentorship guides career development, from setting goals to navigating career transitions. Community involvement offers exposure to diverse experiences and perspectives. The support and encouragement from mentors and community members boost your confidence, enabling you to take on new challenges and pursue your ambitions.

## Building and Scaling Your Network: Practical Steps

To ensure that your network continues to grow and remains a source of value, it's essential to be strategic and intentional. Here's a framework to help you build and scale your network effectively:

**Define Your Goals:** Identify what you want to achieve through networking. This could include finding mentors, discovering job opportunities, learning new skills, or collaborating on projects.

**Identify Key Networks:** Research and list key communities, organisations, and events relevant to your field. This includes professional associations, online forums, industry conferences, and local meetups.

**Engage Consistently:** Regularly participate in discussions, attend events, and contribute to community activities. Consistency helps you stay connected and build meaningful relationships.

**Offer Value:** Approach networking with a mindset of giving. Share your knowledge, offer assistance, and provide support to others. This builds goodwill and strengthens your connections.

**Follow-up:** After meeting someone new, follow up with a message or email. Express your appreciation for the conversation and suggest ways to stay in touch or collaborate.

**Diversify Your Network:** Build a diverse network that includes individuals from different backgrounds, industries, and experience levels. A diverse network provides a broader perspective and more opportunities.

**Leverage Technology:** Use networking platforms like LinkedIn, Meetup, and Eventbrite to find and connect with professionals in your field. Engage with their content and participate in online events and discussions.

**Maintain Relationships:** Stay in touch with your network by periodically checking in, sharing updates, and offering support. Strong relationships are built over time through consistent and meaningful interactions.

**Seek and Provide Feedback:** Actively seek feedback from your network on your work and ideas. Similarly, provide constructive feedback to others. This promotes a culture of mutual growth and learning.

**Be Authentic:** Authenticity is key to building genuine relationships. Be yourself, show genuine interest in others, and approach networking with honesty and integrity.

## Examples and Case Studies

### The Power of a Single Connection

Consider the story of a designer who attended a local design meetup and met an industry veteran. The veteran became a mentor, providing valuable insights and guidance. Over time, this mentor introduced the designer to other industry professionals, leading to collaborative projects and job opportunities. This single connection catalysed career growth, demonstrating the power of networking and mentorship.

### Building a Thriving Community

The Creativee, a community I founded, illustrates the impact of a well-organised and engaged community. By providing a platform for creatives around the world to share their work, exchange ideas, and support each other, The Creativee has become a vibrant hub for learning and collaboration. Regular workshops and events promote a sense of belonging and mutual growth, helping members achieve their professional goals.

## Leveraging Mentorship for Career Growth

To leverage mentorship effectively for career growth, being proactive and strategic is essential. Here are some steps to help you make the most of your mentorship relationships:

**Set Clear Goals:** Define specific, measurable, achievable, relevant, and time-bound (SMART) goals for what you want to achieve through mentorship. This provides direction and focus.

**Communicate Expectations:** Clearly communicate your expectations to your mentor. Discuss the frequency of meetings, preferred communication methods, and focus areas.

**Be Open to Feedback:** Embrace feedback from your mentor, even if it's critical. Constructive criticism is essential for growth and improvement.

**Take the initiative:** Be proactive in seeking advice and support. Don't wait for your mentor to reach out—take the initiative to schedule meetings and follow up on discussions.

**Show Gratitude:** Always express your gratitude for your mentor's time and guidance. A simple thank you can go a long way in building a positive and lasting relationship.

**Apply Learnings:** Implement the advice and insights you receive from your mentor. Demonstrating progress and applying learnings shows your commitment and makes the mentorship more effective.

**Reflect on Progress:** Reflect on your progress regularly and discuss it with your mentor. This will help you stay on track and make necessary adjustments to your goals and approach.

**Give Back:** As you benefit from mentorship, look for ways to give back. This could be by sharing what you have learned with others, mentoring junior designers, or contributing to community initiatives.

## The Impact of Community Engagement

Engaging actively with a community can significantly impact your personal and professional growth. Here's how you can maximise the benefits of community engagement:

**Participate in Events:** Attend community events like workshops, webinars and meetups. These provide opportunities to learn, network, and collaborate with others.

**Contribute to Discussions:** Actively participate in online forums, social media groups, and community discussions. Share your insights, ask questions, and engage with others' content.

**Share Your Work:** Showcase your projects, case studies, and design processes within the community. This will not only provide visibility but also invite feedback and collaboration opportunities.

**Seek Collaboration:** Look for opportunities to collaborate on projects with community members. Collaborative projects enhance your skills, expand your portfolio, and build stronger connections.

**Stay Informed:** Engaging with community content helps you stay relevant and informed about industry trends, news, and developments.

## Giving Back to the Community

One of the most rewarding aspects of being part of a community and having received mentorship is the opportunity to give back. Sharing your knowledge and experiences not only helps others but also reinforces your learning and growth. Here's how you can give back to the community:

**Become a Mentor:** As you gain experience, consider mentoring others. Offer guidance, share your insights, and help others navigate their career paths.

**Share Knowledge:** Write articles, create tutorials, or give talks to share your expertise with the broader community. Your knowledge can inspire and educate others.

**Organise Events:** Take an active role in organising community events, workshops, or meetups. These events provide valuable learning opportunities and foster a sense of community.

**Support New Initiatives:** Support new initiatives within the community by volunteering your time, providing resources, or offering your expertise.

**Participate in Discussions:** Engage in community discussions by providing constructive feedback, sharing insights, and supporting others' ideas.

**Collaborate on Projects:** Work on collaborative projects with community members. This will enhance your skills, expand your portfolio, and build stronger connections.

**Celebrate Successes:** Recognise and celebrate community members' successes. This builds a positive and supportive environment where everyone feels valued and motivated.

## Conclusion: The Power of Mentorship and Community

Mentorship and community are the cornerstones of growth and development in the design world. They provide the guidance, support, and inspiration needed to navigate the challenges and seize the opportunities of a design career. By actively seeking out mentors and engaging with supportive communities, you can unlock new levels of personal and professional growth.

Remember, the journey of growth is not one to be travelled alone. Surround yourself with mentors who inspire you and communities that uplift you. Embrace the power of shared knowledge, collaborative learning, and mutual support. Let mentorship and community be your guiding lights, illuminating the path to your success.

# CHAPTER 6

## Resilience: Standing Up and Facing Defeat

Every creative journey is marked by setbacks and failures. Rather than mere obstacles, these challenges are integral parts of the path to success. Resilience—the ability to bounce back from adversity and persist in challenges—is a crucial trait for any designer. This chapter explores and investigates the essence of resilience, offering practical advice, frameworks, and inspiring stories to help you build the strength to persevere. It's about transforming failures into opportunities for growth and maintaining consistency in your efforts, no matter how tough the journey gets.

### The Nature of Resilience

Resilience is not just about enduring hardships; it's about thriving through adversity. It's the capacity to maintain purpose and integrity despite setbacks and challenges. For designers, resilience means continuously pushing the boundaries of creativity, learning from failures, and remaining committed to your vision. This chapter aims to equip you with the mindset and tools to cultivate resilience, turning every setback into a stepping stone toward success.

## Embracing Failure

Failure is an inevitable part of the creative process. It's important to reframe failure not as a negative outcome but as a valuable learning experience. Each failure teaches us something new, offering insights that can lead to better solutions and innovations. Here are some key points to understand about failure:

**Failure is Universal:** Everyone experiences failure. It's a common thread in successful people's journeys across all fields.

**Failure is a Teacher:** Each failure provides lessons that can inform future actions and decisions. It's an opportunity to better understand what works and what doesn't.

**Failure is Temporary:** Setbacks are not permanent. They are moments in time that provide opportunities for growth and improvement.

**Failure Builds Strength:** Overcoming failure builds mental and emotional strength, preparing you for future challenges.

## Stories of Resilience

### The Persistence of Walt Disney

Walt Disney is synonymous with creativity and innovation, but his journey was fraught with failures.

He was fired from a newspaper for lacking creativity and faced several business failures, including the bankruptcy of his first animation company. Despite these setbacks, Disney persisted. He continued to innovate and eventually created Mickey Mouse, a character that led to the foundation of his empire. Disney's resilience and determination to pursue his vision, despite repeated failures, highlight the importance of perseverance in achieving success.

## The Determination of Elon Musk

Elon Musk, the entrepreneur behind Tesla, SpaceX, and several other groundbreaking ventures, faced significant challenges on his path to success. From Tesla's near bankruptcy to SpaceX's multiple failures of its early rockets, Musk's journey has been anything but smooth. Despite these setbacks, he remained steadfast in his vision. Musk's resilience in the face of adversity has led to remarkable achievements in both the automotive and aerospace industries, demonstrating the power of persistence and unwavering commitment.

## The Resilience of Dr. A.P.J. Abdul Kalam

Before becoming one of India's most revered scientists and the 11th President of India, Dr. A.P.J. Abdul Kalam faced numerous challenges. Growing up in a humble background, he overcame financial difficulties to pursue an education in aerospace engineering. Despite initial failures in missile and space projects, Kalam's resilience remained strong. He led successful projects like India's first satellite launch vehicle and the development of ballistic missiles.

As President, he bridged the gap between science and the public, inspiring millions with his vision for a developed India. Dr Kalam's story is a testament to the power of resilience, demonstrating that determination and hard work can overcome any obstacle and achieve greatness.

## How to Build Resilience

Building resilience requires intentional practice and commitment. Here are some practical steps to help you develop resilience:

**Embrace Challenges:**

- Step out of your comfort zone and take on new challenges.

- View difficulties as opportunities to learn and grow.

- Accept that failure is a part of the process and use it as a learning tool.

**Learn from Failures:**

- Use failure as a stepping stone to success.

- Reflect on your failures and identify the lessons they offer.

- Adjust your strategies and approaches based on these insights.

**Set Realistic Goals:**

- Break down your goals into manageable steps.

- Celebrate small achievements along the way.

- Adjust your goals as needed based on feedback and experiences.

**Stay Consistent:**

- Maintain consistency in your efforts, even when progress seems slow.

- Develop routines and habits that support your goals.

- Recognise that small, consistent actions lead to significant results over time.

**Seek Feedback:**

- Actively seek feedback from mentors, peers, and users.

- Use feedback to refine your work and improve your skills.

- Embrace constructive criticism as an opportunity for growth.

**Develop a Growth Mindset:**

- Believe in your ability to develop and improve through effort and practice.

- Embrace the process of learning and improvement.

- Stay open to new ideas and perspectives.

## Build a Support Network:

- Surround yourself with supportive friends, family, and colleagues.

- Seek advice, encouragement, and feedback from your network.

- Share your struggles and successes with others.

## Frameworks for Resilience

Adopting specific frameworks can help structure your approach to building resilience. Here are two effective frameworks:

## The ABCDE Model

The ABCDE Model is a cognitive-behavioural approach to resilience developed by psychologist Martin Seligman. It helps individuals reframe negative thoughts and create a more positive outlook.

### A - Adversity:

- Identify the adversity or challenge you are facing.

### B - Beliefs:

- Recognise the beliefs you hold about adversity.

- These beliefs often include negative thoughts or assumptions.

### C - Consequences:

- Understand the consequences of these beliefs.

- Negative beliefs can lead to negative emotions and behaviours.

## D - Disputation:

- Dispute and challenge the negative beliefs.

- Replace them with more positive and realistic thoughts.

## E - Energization:

- Experience the positive energy that comes from reframing your beliefs.

- Use this energy to take constructive action.

## The GRIT Framework

Developed by psychologist Angela Duckworth, the GRIT Framework emphasises the importance of perseverance and passion in achieving long-term goals.

- **G - Goals:** Set clear, long-term goals that are meaningful to you.

- **R - Resilience:** Cultivate resilience by embracing challenges and learning from failures.

- **I - Inner Strength:** Develop inner strength by practising self-discipline and maintaining focus.

- **T - Tenacity:** Demonstrate tenacity by persisting through difficulties and staying committed to your goals.

## The Role of Consistency in Building Resilience

Consistency plays a crucial role in building resilience. It's about maintaining steady effort and progress, even in the face of setbacks. Here's how consistency contributes to resilience:

**Builds Habits:**

- Consistent actions lead to the formation of positive habits.

- These habits support your goals and contribute to long-term success.

**Fosters Discipline:**

- Consistency requires discipline and self-control.

- It helps you stay focused and avoid distractions.

**Creates Momentum:**

- Small, consistent actions build momentum over time.

- This momentum drives progress and keeps you moving forward.

**Enhances Skills:**

- Regular practice and effort lead to skill improvement.

- Consistency helps you improve your techniques and become more proficient.

**Builds Confidence:**

- Consistent effort and progress build confidence.

- You develop a belief in your ability to achieve your goals.

## The Importance of a Support Network

A strong support network is essential for building resilience. Surrounding yourself with supportive individuals provides encouragement, advice, and a sense of belonging. Here's how to develop and leverage a support network:

**Identify Key Supporters:**

- Identify friends, family, mentors, and colleagues who can provide support.

- These individuals should be positive, encouraging, and willing to offer help.

**Communicate Openly:**

- Share your goals, challenges, and progress with your support network.

- Open communication fosters trust and understanding.

**Seek Advice and Feedback:**

- Actively seek advice and feedback from your support network.

- Use their insights to improve and refine your approach.

**Offer Support in Return:**

- Support others in their endeavours.

- Offer encouragement, advice, and assistance when needed.

**Stay Connected:**

- Regularly check in with your support network.

- Maintain strong relationships through consistent communication.

## Real-World Applications of Resilience

Resilience is not just a theoretical concept; it has real-world applications that can significantly impact your career and personal life. Here are some practical examples of how resilience can be applied:

**Overcoming Creative Blocks**

Creative blocks are common in the design process. Resilience helps you push through these blocks by maintaining a positive mindset and staying committed to your work. When faced with a creative block, take a break, seek inspiration from different sources, and return to your work with a fresh perspective. Embrace the challenge as an opportunity to explore new ideas and approaches.

## Navigating Career Transitions

Career transitions can be challenging and filled with uncertainty. Resilience helps you navigate these transitions by staying adaptable and open to new opportunities. When changing jobs or career paths, focus on your strengths, seek advice from mentors, and remain optimistic about the future. Use the transition to learn new skills and expand your network.

## Handling Client Rejections

Client rejections are a part of the design industry. Resilience helps you handle these rejections by viewing them as learning experiences. When clients reject your work, seek feedback to understand their concerns and preferences. Use this feedback to improve your designs and better meet client expectations in the future. Maintain a positive attitude and continue to refine your skills.

## The Role of Calmness and Meditation in Building Resilience

Staying calm under pressure is a critical component of resilience. Practising mindfulness and meditation can help you maintain your composure and focus during challenging times. Here's how these practices contribute to resilience:

## Mindfulness:

- Mindfulness involves being fully present in the moment aware of your thoughts and feelings without judgement.

- Practising mindfulness helps you stay grounded and reduces stress and anxiety.

- It improves your ability to respond to challenges with clarity and calmness.

## Meditation:

- Meditation is a practice that involves focused attention and relaxation techniques.

- Regular meditation reduces stress, improves emotional regulation, and enhances concentration.

- It helps you develop a calm and focused mindset, which is essential for navigating adversity.

## Deep Breathing Exercises:

- Deep breathing exercises can quickly calm your mind and body during stressful situations.

- Practising deep breathing helps you maintain composure and make better decisions under pressure.

## Frameworks to Understand Failure and Bounce Back

Understanding failure and learning to bounce back involves structured reflection and action. Here are two frameworks to help you navigate and learn from failures:

### The Failure Analysis Framework

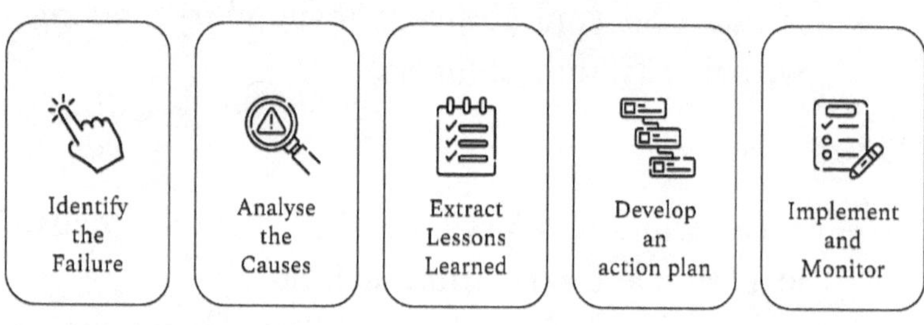


**Identify the Failure:**

- Clearly define the failure or setback you experienced.

- Understand the context and specifics of what went wrong.

**Analyse the Causes:**

- Identify the factors that contributed to the failure.

- Consider internal factors (e.g., skills, decisions) and external factors (e.g., market conditions, team dynamics).

**Extract Lessons Learned:**

- Reflect on the insights gained from the failure.

- Identify what you could have done differently and what you learned about yourself and your work.

**Develop an Action Plan:**

- Create a plan to address the factors that led to the failure.

- Set specific, actionable steps to improve and avoid similar issues in the future.

**Implement and Monitor:**

- Execute your action plan and monitor your progress.

- Regularly review and adjust your plan based on feedback and outcomes.

### The Bounce-Back Framework

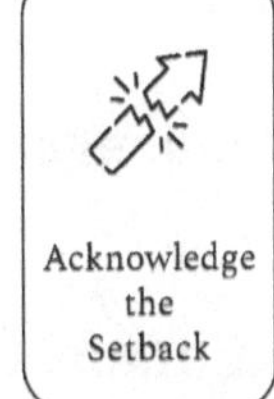

Acknowledge the Setback

Reflect and Reframe

Rebuild the Confidence

Seek Support and Guidance

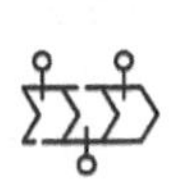

Take Proactive Steps

**Acknowledge the Setback:**

- Accept that setbacks and failures are part of the journey.

- Acknowledgement is the first step toward recovery.

**Reflect and Reframe:**

- Reflect on the experience and reframe your perspective.

- View failure as a learning opportunity rather than a defeat.

**Rebuild Confidence:**

- Focus on your strengths and past successes to rebuild your confidence.

- Set small, achievable goals to regain momentum.

**Seek Support and Guidance:**

- Reach out to your support network for encouragement and advice.

- Use their insights to gain new perspectives and solutions.

**Take Proactive Steps:**

- Develop a proactive plan to address the challenges and move forward.

- Stay committed to your goals and maintain a positive outlook.

## Inspirational Quotes on Resilience

- "Success is not final, failure is not fatal: It is the courage to continue that counts." — Winston Churchill

- "The greatest glory in living lies not in never falling, but in rising every time we fall." — Nelson Mandela

- "Life doesn't get easier or more forgiving, we get stronger and more resilient." — Steve Maraboli

- "It's not whether you get knocked down, it's whether you get up." — Vince Lombardi

## Conclusion: The Power of Resilience

Resilience is the cornerstone of success in the face of adversity. It's about embracing challenges, learning from failures, and consistently working towards your goals. By developing a growth mindset, practising self-compassion, building a support network, and maintaining a positive outlook, you can cultivate resilience and turn setbacks into opportunities for growth.

Remember, resilience is not a destination but a journey. It's about continuously pushing yourself to improve, staying committed to your vision, and persevering through the ups and downs of the creative process. Embrace the power of resilience and let it guide you towards a successful and fulfilling career in design.

# CHAPTER 7

## The Gift of Feedback: Receiving and Growing

Feedback is the cornerstone of growth and improvement. In the design world, where innovation and creativity are paramount, feedback guides us towards better solutions and more refined outcomes. This chapter explores embracing feedback as a valuable tool, providing constructive criticism, and effectively incorporating feedback into your work. With practical frameworks and inspiring stories from the design world, this chapter aims to make giving and receiving feedback both enlightening and empowering.

### The Importance of Feedback

Feedback is essential for several reasons. It provides an external perspective on your work, highlighting areas of improvement you might not see. It also validates your efforts, showing you what works well and resonates with your audience. Additionally, feedback fosters a culture of continuous learning and growth, encouraging you to push your boundaries and strive for excellence.

Feedback comes in various forms, including user feedback, peer reviews, client critiques, and self-assessment. Each type of feedback offers unique insights that contribute to your development as a designer. Embracing feedback means acknowledging its role in your growth and understanding that it is a critical component of the creative process.

## Embracing Feedback

Embracing feedback requires a mindset shift. It's about viewing feedback not as criticism but as an opportunity for growth. Here are some principles to help you embrace feedback:

**Adopt a Growth Mindset:** Believe that your skills and abilities can be developed through effort and learning. This mindset makes you more open to feedback and eager to use it to improve. Embracing a growth mindset involves seeing challenges as opportunities, persisting in the face of setbacks, and finding inspiration in others' successes.

**Be Open and Receptive:** Approach feedback with an open mind. Listen carefully to what is being said without becoming defensive. Understand that feedback is not a personal attack but a tool for improvement. Being open and receptive also means being willing to hear and act on feedback from various sources, including those you might not initially agree with.

**Seek Clarity:** If feedback is vague or unclear, ask questions to better understand it. Clarifying feedback ensures that you can act on it effectively. Understanding the specific context and examples behind the feedback is important to making meaningful improvements.

**Reflect and Evaluate:** Take time to reflect on the feedback you receive. Evaluate its validity and relevance to your work. Consider how the feedback aligns with your goals and objectives, and decide which aspects to prioritise.

**Take Action:** Use feedback as a guide to make improvements. Implement changes and observe their impact on your work. Taking action on feedback demonstrates your commitment to growth and your willingness to improve continuously.

## Providing Constructive Criticism

Providing constructive criticism is an art. It's about offering feedback in a way that is helpful and encouraging rather than discouraging. Here's how to provide constructive criticism effectively:

**Be Specific:** General feedback is less helpful than specific feedback. Highlight particular aspects of the work that need improvement. Provide concrete examples and detailed observations to make your feedback actionable.

**Be Objective:** Focus on the work, not the person. This helps the recipient feel less defensive and more open to your suggestions. Maintaining objectivity ensures that the feedback is received in the spirit of improvement rather than as a personal critique.

**Be Balanced:** Provide a balance of positive and negative feedback. Highlight what is working well before pointing out areas for improvement. A balanced approach helps maintain morale and encourages the recipient to continue building on their strengths while addressing their weaknesses.

**Be Actionable:** Offer suggestions for how to improve. Actionable feedback provides clear guidance on what to do next. Providing practical steps and recommendations makes implementing the feedback more straightforward for the recipient.

**Be Empathetic:** Understand that receiving feedback can be difficult. Offer your criticism with empathy and encouragement. Recognise the effort and intentions behind the work and provide support to help the recipient grow.

## Frameworks for Giving and Receiving Feedback

To make the process of giving and receiving feedback more structured and practical, consider using the following frameworks:

### The SBI Model (Situation-Behavior-Impact)

The SBI Model is a simple yet powerful framework for providing feedback. It focuses on specific situations and behaviours and their impact.

- **Situation:** Describe the specific situation in which the behaviour occurred.

- **Behaviour:** Describe the behaviour you observed.

- **Impact:** Explain the impact of the behaviour on you or others.

**Example:** "During the team meeting (Situation), you interrupted while others were speaking (Behaviour). This made it difficult for others to share their ideas and caused some frustration (Impact)."

**The COIN Model (Context-Observation-Impact-Next Steps)**

The COIN Model is another practical feedback framework. It provides a clear structure for describing the context, observation, impact, and next steps.

- **Context:** Set context for feedback.

- **Observation:** Describe what you observed.

- **Impact:** Explain the impact of the observation.

- **Next Steps:** Suggest the next steps or actions to take.

**Example:** "In our recent project review (Context), I noticed that the presentation lacked a clear structure (Observation). This made it difficult for stakeholders to track our progress (Impact). I suggest we outline the key points before our next presentation (Next Steps)."

## The Impact of Feedback on the Design World

Feedback has shaped the design world in profound ways. Here are some inspiring stories of how feedback has driven innovation and improvement in design:

### Story 1: The Evolution of the iPhone

The development of the iPhone is a testament to the power of feedback. During the design and testing phases, Apple's design team received extensive feedback from internal teams and beta testers. This feedback highlighted issues with the initial designs, leading to significant improvements. For instance, feedback on the touchscreen sensitivity and user interface led to refinements that made the iPhone more user-friendly and intuitive. The iterative process of incorporating feedback was crucial to the iPhone's success and its evolution into one of the most iconic products in tech history.

### Story 2: Airbnb's User Experience Overhaul

Airbnb's transformation from a struggling startup to a global hospitality giant is a story deeply rooted in feedback. In the early days, the founders personally visited hosts to gather feedback on their experiences. They discovered that many hosts struggled with taking quality photos of their listings. In response, Airbnb launched a professional photography program, significantly improving the user experience. This initiative, driven by feedback, was pivotal in Airbnb's growth and success.

### Story 3: The Revamp of Gmail

Gmail's interface has undergone several changes since its launch, many driven by user feedback. Google's design team regularly gathers feedback through surveys, user testing, and community forums. When users expressed frustration with the cluttered interface and difficulty managing emails, Google introduced features like tabs and smart categorization. These feedback- based changes have made Gmail more efficient and user-friendly.

## Practical Steps to Incorporate Feedback

Incorporating feedback effectively involves more than just listening to suggestions. Here are practical steps to help you incorporate feedback into your work:

**Listen Actively:** Pay close attention to the feedback you receive. Avoid interrupting and show that you value the input.

**Take Notes:** Write down the feedback to ensure you don't miss any critical points. It also shows you take feedback seriously.

**Clarify and Ask Questions:** If any part of the feedback is unclear, ask questions to gain clarity. Understanding the feedback fully is crucial for effective implementation.

**Reflect on the Feedback:** Take time to reflect on the feedback. Consider its validity and relevance to your work.

**Prioritise Actions:** Identify the most important pieces of feedback and prioritise actions. Focus on making changes that will have the most significant impact.

**Implement Changes:** Develop a plan to implement the feedback. Make the necessary changes and monitor the results.

**Seek Follow-Up Feedback:** After making changes, seek follow-up feedback to ensure effective improvements. This ongoing process helps you continue to refine and enhance your work.

## Creating a Feedback-Friendly Culture

Creating a culture where feedback is valued and encouraged is essential for continuous improvement. Here's how to foster a feedback-friendly environment:

**Lead by Example:** As a leader, demonstrate that you value feedback by actively seeking and acting on it.

**Encourage Open Communication:** Create an environment where team members feel comfortable sharing their thoughts and ideas. Encourage open and honest communication.

**Provide Training:** Offer training on how to give and receive feedback effectively. Equip your team with the skills they need to provide constructive criticism.

**Recognise and Reward:** Recognize and reward team members who provide valuable feedback. Show appreciation for their contributions.

**Create Feedback Opportunities:** Integrate feedback opportunities into regular workflows. Use meetings, reviews, and retrospectives as platforms for sharing feedback.

**Follow Through:** Show that you take feedback seriously by acting on it and making necessary changes. Following through demonstrates that feedback is valued and impactful.

## Overcoming Feedback Resistance

Feedback resistance is common but can be overcome with the right approach. Here are strategies to help you overcome feedback resistance:

**Understand the Resistance:** Identify the reasons for resistance. Is it fear of criticism, lack of trust, or past negative experiences?

**Build Trust:** Establish a foundation of trust with the individuals to whom you provide feedback. Trust is essential for feedback to be received openly.

**Provide Context:** Explain the purpose and importance of the feedback. Providing context helps the recipient understand its value.

**Be Empathetic:** Show empathy and understanding. Acknowledge that receiving feedback can be challenging and offer support.

**Use Positive Reinforcement:** Highlight positive aspects before addressing areas of improvement. Positive reinforcement can make feedback more palatable.

**Encourage Self-Reflection:** Encourage individuals to reflect on their performance and identify areas for improvement. Self-reflection can make feedback more meaningful.

## Inspirational Stories of Feedback

Incorporating real-world stories of how feedback has transformed the design world can provide powerful insights and motivation:

### The Power of User Feedback in Design

User feedback is invaluable in the design process. It provides insights into how real users interact with products and highlights areas for improvement. For instance, the redesign of Instagram's interface was heavily influenced by user feedback. Users expressed frustration with the complexity of certain features, leading the design team to simplify the interface and enhance usability. This user-centred approach, driven by feedback, contributed to Instagram's continued growth and popularity.

### Pixar's Braintrust

Pixar Animation Studios is renowned for its creative excellence, and feedback plays a crucial role in their success. Pixar's "Braintrust" is a group of directors and storytellers who provide candid feedback on each other's work. This iterative feedback process ensures that every story element is refined and polished. The constructive criticism from the Braintrust has helped Pixar create some of the most beloved animated films of all time, such as "Toy Story," "Finding Nemo," and "Up."

## IDEO's Feedback Culture

IDEO, a global design and innovation consultancy, is known for its strong feedback culture. IDEO encourages a collaborative environment where feedback is integral to the design process. Team members regularly seek and provide feedback, fostering a culture of continuous improvement. This approach has led to groundbreaking innovations in various industries, from healthcare to consumer products.

## The Transformative Power of Feedback

Feedback has the power to transform not just individual projects, but entire careers and industries. When designers embrace feedback as a tool for growth, they unlock new levels of creativity and innovation. Here are some additional ways feedback can be transformative:

### Enhancing Creativity

Feedback provides new perspectives and ideas that can spark creativity. By considering different viewpoints and suggestions, designers can explore new directions and approaches they might not have considered. This collaborative process often leads to more innovative and creative solutions.

### Improving Collaboration

A feedback-friendly culture fosters better collaboration among team members. When everyone feels comfortable sharing their thoughts and ideas, it creates an environment of mutual respect and trust. This collaborative spirit enhances teamwork and leads to better outcomes.

## Accelerating Learning

Feedback accelerates the learning process by providing immediate insights into what works and what doesn't. This real-time learning allows designers to make adjustments and improvements quickly, leading to faster development and higher-quality results.

## Building Confidence

Receiving constructive feedback and acting on it can boost a designer's confidence. Knowing that you can handle criticism and use it to improve your work reinforces your belief in your abilities and resilience in the face of challenges.

## Strengthening Client Relationships

Providing and receiving feedback is crucial in client relationships. Clients appreciate when designers are open to feedback and willing to make adjustments based on their input. This collaborative approach builds trust and strengthens the relationship, leading to more successful projects and satisfied clients.

## Conclusion: The Gift of Feedback

Feedback is a powerful tool for growth and improvement. By embracing feedback with an open mind, providing constructive criticism with empathy, and effectively incorporating feedback into your work, you can elevate your design practice to new heights. Creating a feedback-friendly culture, overcoming resistance, and learning from real-world examples can transform how you view and utilise feedback.

Remember, feedback is a gift. It provides valuable insights, highlights areas for improvement, and validates your efforts. Embrace the gift of feedback and let it guide you on your journey to becoming a better designer and a more effective communicator.

# CHAPTER 8

## Crafting Your Legacy: Building a Personal Brand as a Designer

In today's competitive market, building a personal brand is essential for designers to stand out, attract opportunities, and advance their careers. A solid personal brand communicates your unique value, expertise, and professional identity. This chapter explores the importance of personal branding, strategies for building and maintaining your brand, and how to leverage your brand for career growth.

### The Importance of Personal Branding

Your brand is your professional identity and reputation. It encompasses your skills, values, and the unique perspective you bring to your work. A strong personal brand can:

**Differentiate You from Others:** A distinctive personal brand sets you apart from other designers in a crowded marketplace. It highlights your unique strengths and makes you more memorable to potential clients and employers.

**Build Trust and Credibility:** A well-defined personal brand establishes you as an authority in your field. It builds trust with your audience and demonstrates your expertise, making you the go-to person for specific skills or knowledge.

**Attract Opportunities:** A solid personal brand can attract job offers, freelance projects, speaking engagements, and other professional opportunities. It makes you more visible to those seeking your skills and expertise.

**Support Career Growth:** A clear and compelling personal brand can help you advance your career by positioning you for promotions, raises, and leadership roles. It communicates your value to your current and future employers.

## Strategies for Building Your Personal Brand

Building a personal brand requires intentional effort and consistency. Here are some strategies to help you create and maintain a solid personal brand:

**Define Your Brand Identity:** Identify your unique strengths, skills, and values. Consider what sets you apart from other designers and what you want to be known for. Create a brand statement that succinctly communicates your professional identity and value proposition.

**Create a Professional Online Presence:** Your online presence is crucial to your personal brand. Develop a professional website or portfolio that showcases your work, skills, and accomplishments. Use social media platforms like LinkedIn, Twitter, and Instagram to share your insights and projects and connect with others in the industry.

**Share Your Expertise:** Establish yourself as an authority by sharing your knowledge and expertise. Write articles, blog posts, and case studies on topics related to your field. Participate in industry forums, webinars, and conferences. Sharing your insights builds your reputation and demonstrates your commitment to continuous learning and professional development.

**Network and Build Relationships:** Networking is essential for building your personal brand. Attend industry events, join professional organisations, and connect with peers, mentors, and potential clients. Building strong relationships can lead to valuable collaborations, referrals, and opportunities.

**Seek Feedback and Refine Your Brand:** Regularly seek feedback from peers, mentors, and clients to understand how your brand is perceived. Use this feedback to refine and strengthen your brand. Stay true to your core values and adapt your brand to reflect your growth and evolving goals.

**Be Consistent:** Consistency is key to maintaining a strong personal brand. Ensure that your messaging, visual identity, and professional behaviour align with your brand across all platforms and interactions. Consistent branding builds trust and reinforces your professional identity.

## Building an Authentic Brand

Authenticity is the cornerstone of a strong personal brand. An authentic brand resonates with people and builds genuine connections. Here's how to create an authentic personal brand:

**Be True to Yourself:** Authenticity starts with self-awareness. Understand your values, strengths, and passions. Your personal brand should reflect who you are and what you stand for. Avoid trying to be someone you're not or emulating others' brands. Authenticity shines through when you are genuine to yourself.

**Share Your Story:** Your personal story is a powerful tool for building an authentic brand. Share your journey, experiences, and lessons learned. Be open about your successes and challenges. Your story makes you relatable and helps others connect with you more deeply.

**Show Your Personality:** Don't be afraid to let your personality shine through in your branding. Your personality adds a unique flavour to your brand, whether serious, humorous, or somewhere in between. It makes you memorable and helps you stand out.

**Be Transparent:** Transparency builds trust. Be honest about your capabilities, experiences, and intentions. If you make a mistake, own it and learn from it. Transparency fosters credibility and strengthens your brand's authenticity.

**Engage Authentically:** Genuinely and meaningfully engage with your audience. Respond to comments, messages, and feedback with sincerity. Show appreciation for your supporters and build relationships based on mutual respect and authenticity.

## Framework for Building Your Personal Brand

To help you build a solid personal brand, here's a step-by-step framework:

**Self-Assessment:**

- **Identify Your Strengths:** List your key skills, talents, and areas of expertise.

- **Define Your Values:** Identify the core values that guide your actions and decisions.

- **Determine Your Passion:** Understand what drives you and what you are passionate about.

**Brand Positioning:**

- **Create a Brand Statement:** Craft a concise statement summarising who you are, what you do, and what makes you unique.

- **Identify Your Target Audience:** Determine who you want to reach and influence with your brand.

**Brand Development:**

- **Develop Your Visual Identity:** Create a consistent visual identity, including a logo, colour scheme, and typography.

- **Build Your Online Presence:** Develop a professional website or portfolio and establish profiles on relevant social media platforms.

- **Content Creation:** Share valuable content that showcases your expertise and insights. This could include blog posts, articles, videos, and case studies.

**Brand Communication:**

- **Networking:** Attend industry events, join professional organisations, and connect with peers, mentors, and potential clients.

- **Engagement:** Actively engage with your audience by responding to comments, messages, and feedback.

- **Public Speaking:** Seek opportunities to speak at conferences, webinars, and industry events to share your knowledge and build your brand.

**Brand Monitoring and Refinement:**

- **Seek Feedback:** Regularly seek feedback from peers, mentors, and clients to understand how your brand is perceived.

- **Monitor Your Online Presence:** Use tools like Google Alerts and social media analytics to monitor your online presence and track your brand's performance.

- **Continuous Improvement:** Use feedback and analytics to refine and strengthen your brand.

Stay true to your core values and adapt your brand to reflect your growth and evolving goals.

## Leveraging Your Brand for Career Growth

Once you have established a solid personal brand, leverage it to advance your career and achieve your professional goals:

**Highlight Your Brand in Job Applications:** Use your personal brand to enhance your job applications. Tailor your resume, cover letter, and portfolio to reflect your brand identity and value proposition. Emphasise your unique strengths and achievements that align with the job requirements.

**Negotiate with Confidence:** A solid personal brand can boost your confidence during salary negotiations and job offers. Use your brand to demonstrate your value and justify your compensation expectations. Highlight your expertise, accomplishments, and the impact you can bring to the organisation.

**Seek Leadership Roles:** Leverage your brand to position yourself for leadership opportunities. Highlight your ability to lead, mentor, and inspire others. Showcase your strategic thinking, decision-making skills, and contributions to successful projects.

**Expand Your Reach:** Use your brand to expand your reach and influence. Pursue speaking engagements, guest lectures, and media appearances. Share your insights and experiences with a broader audience to build your reputation and attract new opportunities.

**Build a Personal Brand Legacy:** Think long-term and consider the legacy you want to leave. Aim to build a personal brand that evolves with you and continues to make an impact throughout your career. Focus on creating a lasting impression that reflects your values, contributions, and influence in the design industry.

## Real-Life Examples of Successful Personal Brands

To illustrate the power of personal branding, let's explore some examples of designers who have successfully built strong personal brands:

### Jessica Walsh

Jessica Walsh's personal brand epitomises the power of authenticity and individuality. As a renowned designer and co-founder of the design agency &Walsh, she has carved a niche with her bold and colourful style. Her fearless approach to self-expression defines her work and inspires others to embrace their uniqueness. Jessica's journey is a testament to the impact of staying true to oneself, showcasing that authenticity can lead to remarkable success and influence in the design industry.

### Aaron Draplin

Aaron Draplin, founder of Draplin Design Co., is celebrated for his distinctive design style and engaging personality. His personal brand revolves around his genuine passion for design, storytelling, and authenticity. Aaron's unique approach and dedication have attracted high-profile clients and a loyal following. His story demonstrates the importance of staying passionate and authentic, illustrating how these qualities can create a compelling personal brand and foster deep connections with audiences.

**Debbie Millman**

Debbie Millman is a designer, author, and host of the acclaimed podcast Design Matters. Her personal brand is rooted in her extensive branding expertise, insightful interviews with industry leaders, and unwavering commitment to fostering creativity. Debbie's dedication to her craft has positioned her as a thought leader and influencer in the design community. Her journey underscores the significance of expertise, continuous learning, and the ability to inspire others, proving that a solid personal brand can elevate one's influence and impact.

## Conclusion: Crafting Your Legacy

Building a personal brand is an ongoing journey that requires self-awareness, intentional effort, and consistency. By defining your unique strengths, creating a professional online presence, sharing your expertise, and engaging authentically with your audience, you can build a strong personal brand that sets you apart and opens doors to new opportunities.

Remember, your personal brand is more than just a marketing tool—it reflects who you are and the legacy you want to leave in the design industry. Embrace your authenticity, share your story, and continuously refine your brand to reflect your growth and evolving goals.

Your personal brand is a powerful asset that can propel you towards a successful and fulfilling career. Embrace the process, stay true to yourself, and let your unique voice shine through in everything you do.

# CHAPTER 9

## Leading with Purpose: Design Leadership and Values

Design leadership goes beyond managing projects. It is about inspiring and guiding teams to create meaningful and impactful work. Effective design leadership fosters a culture of innovation, empowers team members, and upholds core values that drive creativity and excellence. This chapter roots into the essential principles of design leadership, strategies for building effective teams, and the importance of fostering a culture of innovation. Through frameworks and examples from leading design studios and inspiring founders, we will explore how to lead purposefully and create a lasting impact.

### The Core Values of Design Leadership

Outstanding design leadership is rooted in core values that guide decision-making and influence the team's culture. These values include:

**Integrity:** Upholding honesty and strong moral principles in all aspects of work. Integrity builds trust within the team and with clients, creating a foundation for successful collaborations.

Empathy is understanding and valuing the perspectives of others. It enables leaders to connect with their team members, clients, and end-users, fostering a more inclusive and user-centred design process.

**Innovation:** Encouraging creativity and the pursuit of new ideas. Innovation drives the design process forward, leading to groundbreaking solutions and advancements.

**Collaboration:** Promoting teamwork and sharing ideas. Collaboration leverages team members' diverse skills and insights, resulting in more prosperous and more effective design outcomes.

**Resilience:** It is the ability to maintain perseverance and adaptability when facing challenges. It helps teams navigate setbacks and keep striving for excellence.

**Vision:** Providing a clear and inspiring direction for the team. Vision aligns efforts and motivates team members to work towards a common goal.

## Building Effective Teams

An effective design team is the cornerstone of successful projects. Building such a team involves strategic recruitment, fostering a collaborative environment, and supporting continuous growth. Here are key strategies for creating and nurturing effective design teams:

**Recruit Diverse Talent:** Diversity in skills, backgrounds, and perspectives enriches the design process. Recruit team members with complementary strengths to create a well-rounded team.

**Foster a Collaborative Culture:** Encourage open communication, idea sharing, and mutual support. A collaborative culture ensures all voices are heard and valued.

**Support Continuous Learning:** Invest in your team members' professional development. Provide opportunities for training, workshops, and conferences to keep their skills sharp and current.

**Empower Autonomy:** Trust your team members to take ownership of their work. Empowering autonomy fosters creativity and innovation while building confidence and accountability.

**Provide Clear Goals and Feedback:** Set clear expectations and provide regular feedback. Constructive feedback helps team members grow and improve, while clear goals keep the team focused and aligned.

**Recognise and Celebrate Achievements:** Acknowledge your team's hard work and successes. Celebrating achievements boosts morale and motivation.

## Frameworks for Effective Design Leadership

To lead with purpose and drive meaningful outcomes, consider adopting the following frameworks:

## The SERVANT Leadership Model

The SERVANT Leadership Model emphasises serving others as the primary goal of leadership. This approach is particularly effective in design, where empathy and collaboration are critical.

### The SERVANT Leadership Model

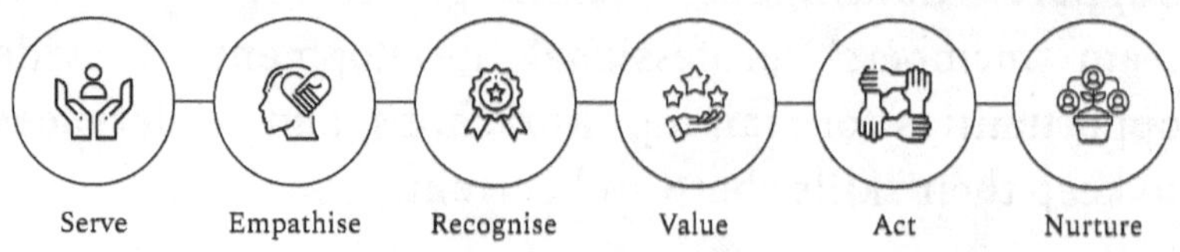


- **Serve:** Focus on serving the needs of your team and clients. Prioritise their well-being and success.

- **Empathise:** Understand and empathise with others' perspectives and challenges. Use empathy to guide your decisions and actions.

- **Recognise:** Recognize your team members' contributions and strengths. Acknowledge their efforts and provide growth opportunities.

- **Value:** Value your team's diversity and unique talents. Leverage these strengths to create better design outcomes.

- **Act:** Take action to support your team and clients. Be proactive in addressing challenges and seizing opportunities.

- **Nurture:** Nurture the development of your team members by providing mentorship, training, and resources to help them grow.

## The Design Thinking Leadership Framework

The Design Thinking Leadership Framework integrates design thinking principles into leadership practices. It emphasises empathy, experimentation, and collaboration.

- **Empathise:** Understand your team's and clients' needs and experiences. Use empathy to inform your leadership approach.

- **Define:** Clearly define the vision, goals, and challenges. Provide a clear direction for your team to follow.

- **Ideate:** Foster a creative environment where team members feel encouraged to generate and share ideas. Facilitate brainstorming sessions and collaborative problem-solving.

- **Prototype:** Encourage experimentation and prototyping. Allow your team to test ideas and learn from failures.

- **Test:** Gather feedback on prototypes and iterate based on insights. Use feedback to refine and improve solutions.

- **Implement:** Lead the implementation of successful solutions. Ensure the end results align with the vision and goals.

## Fostering a Culture of Innovation

Creating a culture of innovation involves nurturing an environment where creativity and experimentation are encouraged. Here's how to foster such a culture:

**Encourage Risk-Taking:** Create a safe space for experimentation. Encourage team members to take risks and explore new ideas without fear of failure.

**Promote Open Communication:** Foster an environment where open communication is valued. Encourage team members to freely share ideas and feedback.

**Provide Resources and Support:** Ensure your team has the tools, resources, and support needed to innovate. Invest in technology, training, and collaborative spaces.

**Celebrate Creativity:** Recognize and celebrate creative ideas and solutions. Highlight the importance of innovation in achieving the team's goals.

**Lead by Example:** Through your actions, demonstrate a commitment to innovation. Show enthusiasm for new ideas and a willingness to embrace change.

## Inspiring Examples of Design Leadership

To understand the impact of effective design leadership, let's explore some inspiring examples from leading design studios and founders around the world:

### IDEO: Pioneering Design Thinking

IDEO, a global design and innovation consultancy, is renowned for its pioneering approach to design thinking.

Founded by David Kelley, IDEO's leadership emphasises empathy, collaboration, and human-centred design. IDEO's innovative projects, such as the first Apple mouse and the shopping cart redesign, demonstrate the power of integrating empathy and creativity into the design process. IDEO's leadership fosters a culture of experimentation and continuous learning, enabling the company to stay at the forefront of design innovation.

IDEO's approach is rooted in the belief that everyone is creative and that innovation comes from collective problem-solving. Their open and inclusive culture encourages team members to bring their whole selves to work, fostering a sense of belonging and shared purpose. By prioritising human-centred design, IDEO has developed solutions that meet user needs, inspire, and delight.

## Pentagram: A Collaborative Collective

Pentagram is one of the world's most prestigious design studios, known for its collaborative approach. Founded in

1972, Pentagram operates as a collective of independent partners, each with their own area of expertise. This unique leadership structure allows for diverse perspectives and creative freedom. Pentagram's iconic projects, including the branding for Mastercard and the signage for The New York Times Building, showcase the studio's commitment to excellence and innovation.

At Pentagram, collaboration is at the core of the design process. Partners work closely with clients and each other to explore ideas, challenge assumptions, and create impactful solutions. This collaborative ethos is reflected in their work, which spans a wide range of disciplines and industries. Pentagram's success demonstrates the power of combining diverse talents and perspectives to achieve outstanding results.

## Airbnb: Redefining Hospitality

Airbnb's journey from a struggling startup to a global leader in hospitality is a testament to visionary design leadership. Co-founders Brian Chesky, Joe Gebbia, and Nathan Blecharczyk emphasised a user-centred approach, gathering feedback directly from hosts and guests to inform their design decisions. Airbnb's leadership prioritised creating a seamless and intuitive user experience, resulting in a platform that revolutionised the travel industry. Their commitment to innovation and empathy has been instrumental in Airbnb's success.

Airbnb's leadership recognised the importance of building trust within its community. Implementing features such as secure payments, verified profiles, and user reviews created a platform that promotes trust and safety. This focus on trust and community has been vital to Airbnb's growth and success. The company's ability to adapt and innovate in response to user feedback has kept it at the forefront of the sharing economy.

## The Role of Design Founders in Shaping the Industry

Design founders play a crucial role in shaping the design industry by setting their organisations' vision, culture, and direction. Their leadership and values influence their own companies and the broader design community. Here are some inspiring design founders who have made a significant impact:

### Jonathan Ive: Apple's Design Visionary

As the former Chief Design Officer at Apple, Jonathan Ive was instrumental in shaping the company's iconic design language. Ive's leadership and vision guided the design of groundbreaking products like the iPhone, iPad, and MacBook. His emphasis on simplicity, elegance, and user experience set new standards for product design and influenced countless designers worldwide. Ive's legacy at Apple demonstrates the power of visionary design leadership in creating products that resonate with users on an emotional level.

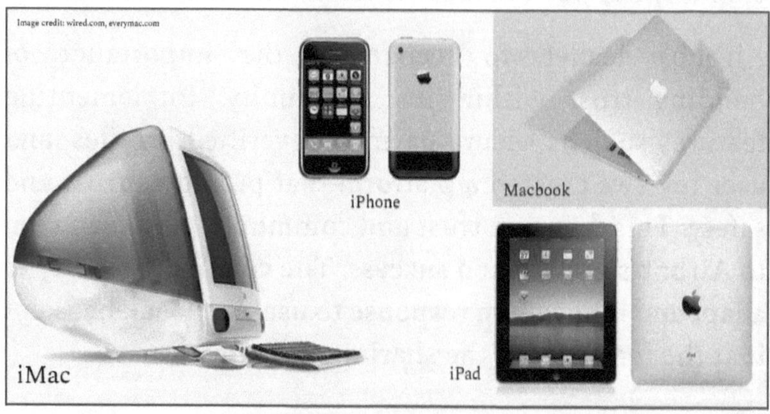


His belief in the power of simplicity deeply influenced Ive's approach to design. He often said simplicity is not about the absence of clutter but bringing order to complexity. This philosophy is evident in Apple's products, known for their intuitive interfaces and elegant aesthetics. Ive's leadership at Apple exemplifies how a clear design vision and commitment to quality and user experience can transform an industry.

## Paula Scher: Pioneering Graphic Design

Paula Scher, a partner at Pentagram, is a pioneer in graphic design. Her work spans iconic branding projects for institutions such as The Public Theater, Citibank, and Microsoft. Scher's leadership and innovative approach have redefined graphic design, blending art and typography to create impactful visual identities. Her commitment to mentorship and education has also inspired a new generation of designers, reinforcing the importance of leadership in nurturing talent.

Scher's design philosophy is rooted in the belief that design should be both functional and beautiful. She has a knack for creating bold, memorable, and effective visual identities. Her work is characterised by its playful use of typography and colour, which has set new standards in the field of graphic design. Scher's leadership at Pentagram and her influence as an educator demonstrate the significant impact that design leaders can have on the industry and on future generations of designers.

## Dieter Rams: Principles of Good Design

Dieter Rams, the legendary designer behind Braun's iconic products, is renowned for his principles of good design. Rams' leadership emphasised functionality, simplicity, and sustainability, which continue to influence modern design. His work at Braun set a benchmark for product design, with his minimalist aesthetic and focus on user experience becoming a timeless reference. Rams' leadership and design philosophy underscores the lasting impact that design founders can have on the industry.

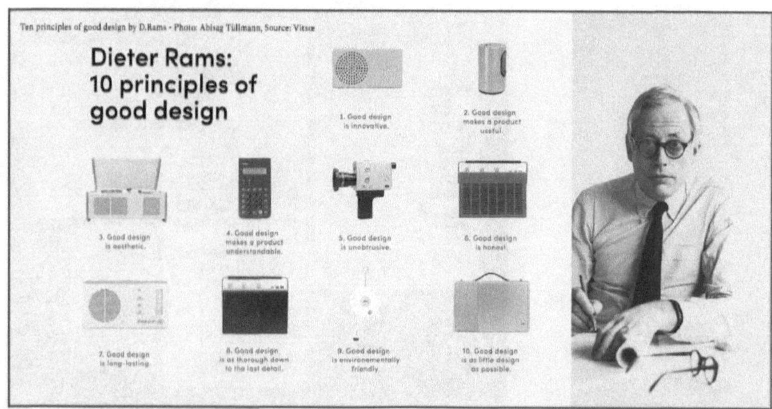


Rams' ten principles of good design, which include being innovative, functional, aesthetic, and environmentally friendly, have become a foundational guideline for designers worldwide. His commitment to these principles ensured that every product he designed was visually pleasing, highly functional, and durable. Rams' approach to design leadership emphasises the importance of maintaining a clear and consistent vision. His work inspires designers to prioritise quality and sustainability in their creations.

## Practical Steps for Design Leadership

**Define Your Vision:** Articulate a clear and inspiring vision for your team. Your vision should provide direction and motivation, aligning the team's efforts towards a common goal.

**Empower Your Team:** Trust your team members to take ownership of their work. Empower them to make decisions and contribute their unique perspectives.

**Foster Collaboration:** Create opportunities for collaboration and idea sharing. Facilitate workshops, brainstorming sessions, and cross-functional projects to leverage your team's collective expertise.

**Encourage Innovation:** Cultivate a culture that encourages creativity and experimentation. Provide your team with the resources and support to explore new ideas and take risks.

**Provide Continuous Feedback:** Offer regular feedback to your team members. Use constructive criticism to guide their growth and recognise their achievements to boost morale.

**Invest in Professional Development:** Support your team's continuous learning and development by providing access to training, conferences, and mentorship opportunities to keep their skills current and sharp.

**Lead by Example:** Demonstrate the values and behaviours you expect from your team. Your actions set the standard and influence your team's culture.

## The Future of Design Leadership

The landscape of design leadership is continuously evolving. As new technologies and methodologies emerge, design leaders must adapt and innovate to stay relevant. Here are some trends shaping the future of design leadership:

**Embracing Digital Transformation:** Design leaders must navigate the complexities of digital transformation. Integrating new technologies such as artificial intelligence, virtual reality, and blockchain into the design process.

**Fostering Inclusivity and Diversity:** Inclusive design and diversity are becoming increasingly important. Design leaders must prioritise creating environments where diverse perspectives are valued and integrated into the design process.

**Sustainability and Ethical Design:** Sustainability and ethical considerations are critical in modern design. Leaders must champion sustainable practices and consider the broader impact of their designs on society and the environment.

**Remote and Distributed Teams:** The rise of remote and distributed teams presents new challenges and opportunities for design leadership. Leaders must find ways to maintain collaboration, communication, and a strong team culture in a remote work environment.

## Conclusion: Leading with Purpose

Design leadership is more than managing projects; it's about inspiring and guiding teams to create meaningful and impactful work. By upholding core values, building effective teams, fostering a culture of innovation, and learning from the examples of visionary design leaders, you can lead with purpose and drive meaningful outcomes.

Remember, leadership in design is not just about the end product; it's about the journey, the collaboration, and the continuous pursuit of excellence. Embrace the role of a design leader with empathy, integrity, and vision. Inspire your team to reach new heights of creativity and innovation.

# CHAPTER 10

## The Intersection of Art and Design: Blurring the Lines

Art and design are often perceived as distinct disciplines, yet they intersect in numerous ways, creating a dynamic and fertile ground for creativity and innovation. This chapter dives into how artistic principles can enhance design practice, the benefits of interdisciplinary collaboration, and what we can learn from the rich history of art. By exploring these intersections, we can gain deeper insights and elevate our design work to new heights.

### The Intersection of Art and Design

Art and design share common goals: communicating, evoking emotions, and creating impactful experiences. However, their methods and contexts can differ. Art often focuses on personal expression and conceptual exploration, while design is typically more functional and user-centred. Despite these differences, the principles and techniques of art can significantly enhance design practice, fostering innovation and creative thinking.

One of the guests on my podcast, Nodes of Design, a renowned artist who transitioned into design, shared an enlightening perspective: "Art is the soul, and design is the body. Art gives design its spirit, passion and depth. When you infuse design with artistic principles, you create something that resonates on a deeper level."

## Artistic Principles in Design

Incorporating artistic principles into design can lead to more innovative and aesthetically pleasing outcomes. Here are some key artistic principles that can enhance design practice:

**Composition and Balance:** Art teaches us the importance of composition and balance. These principles help create visually harmonious designs that guide the viewer's eye and enhance user experience. Just like in a painting where the arrangement of elements can evoke a sense of harmony or tension, design can use these principles to create a flow that guides users effortlessly.

**Colour Theory:** Understanding colour theory is crucial in both art and design. Artists use colour to convey mood and emotion, and designers can apply these principles to create more engaging and effective visual communications. A designer I interviewed emphasised, "Colour is not just decoration; it's communication. It's about the emotions you evoke and the messages you send."

**Texture and Depth:** Art often explores texture and depth to add richness and complexity. Incorporating these elements into the design can create more tactile and immersive experiences. For example, using textured backgrounds or layered elements can give digital designs a sense of tangibility and realism.

**Form and Space:** Artists manipulate form and space to create dynamic and exciting compositions. Designers can use these techniques to organise content and create visual hierarchies. Think of how negative space in a painting can draw attention to the subject; similarly, in design, the strategic use of space can highlight key elements and improve readability.

**Expression and Emotion:** Art is a powerful medium for expressing emotions. We can create more resonant and impactful experiences by integrating expressive elements into design. A design leader on my podcast once said, "Design without emotion is just decoration. It's the emotional connection that makes design memorable and meaningful."

## The Benefits of Interdisciplinary Collaboration

Collaboration between artists and designers can lead to groundbreaking innovations and unique solutions. Here are some benefits of interdisciplinary collaboration:

**Diverse Perspectives:** Artists and designers bring different perspectives and problem-solving approaches. Combining these viewpoints can lead to more creative and comprehensive solutions. For instance, an artist's abstract thinking ability can complement a designer's focus on functionality.

**Example:** Apple's collaboration between industrial designers and artists led to the creation of the iconic Apple products. The seamless integration of form and function in products like the iPhone and MacBook showcases how diverse perspectives can lead to elegant, user-friendly designs. The combination of Steve Jobs' vision and Jony Ive's design expertise resulted in products that revolutionised technology and consumer electronics.

**Enhanced Creativity:** Working with artists can inspire designers to think outside the box and explore new creative territories. This can lead to more innovative and original designs. One of my guests mentioned, "Collaborating with artists pushes you to break out of your comfort zone and see things from a completely different angle."

**Example:** Nike's collaboration with artist Tom Sachs for the Mars Yard Shoe combines Sachs' artistic vision with Nike's advanced design and technology. This partnership resulted in a unique product that challenges traditional design aesthetics and pushes the boundaries of creativity in footwear.

**Cross-Pollination of Ideas:** Interdisciplinary collaboration fosters exchanging ideas and techniques, enriching both fields. Designers can learn new artistic techniques, while artists can gain insights into user-centred design. This cross-pollination can result in aesthetically pleasing and highly functional work.

**Example:** BMW's Art Car Project, where artists like Andy Warhol and Jeff Koons were invited to design car exteriors. These collaborations brought new artistic perspectives into the automotive industry, blending art with engineering and design.

**Expanded Skill Sets:** Collaborating with artists allows designers to develop new skills and expand their creative toolkit. This can enhance their versatility and adaptability in different design contexts. An artist shared on my podcast, "Working with designers taught me to think about the user experience, which has profoundly influenced my art."

**Example:** IKEA's collaboration with fashion designer Virgil Abloh for the "MARKERAD" collection blended high fashion with functional furniture design. Working with Abloh helped IKEA's designers expand their understanding of fashion trends and incorporate them into home furnishings, leading to innovative products that appeal to a broader audience.

**Richer Experiences:** Integrating artistic elements into design can create more engaging and immersive experiences for users, elevating the overall impact and effectiveness of the design. For example, incorporating hand-drawn illustrations or unique artistic styles into a digital interface can make it stand out and resonate more deeply with users.

**Example:** Spotify's collaboration with visual artists for the "Canvas" feature, where short looping videos accompany music tracks. Integrating visual art into the listening experience creates a more immersive and engaging platform for users, enhancing how people interact with music.

These examples demonstrate how interdisciplinary collaboration between artists and designers can lead to groundbreaking innovations and unique solutions that enrich both fields and create more engaging, impactful user experiences.

## Lessons from Art History

Art history is a treasure trove of inspiration and knowledge. By studying the works of great artists and movements, designers can gain valuable insights that inform and enhance their practice. Here are some crucial lessons from art history:

**The Power of Simplicity:** The minimalist works of artists like Kazimir Malevich and Piet Mondrian teach us the power of simplicity. Stripping down designs to their essential elements can create clarity and impact. As one of my guests said, "Simplicity is the ultimate sophistication. It's about making the complex appear effortless."

Aeroplane Flying, 1915.
Kazimir Malevich

Composition A
Piet-Mondrian



**The Use of Symbolism:** Artists like René Magritte and Frida Kahlo used symbolism to convey deeper meanings. Designers can use symbols and metaphors to communicate complex ideas in a visually engaging way. For instance, using an hourglass icon to represent time or a heart to symbolise love can convey meaning quickly and effectively.

Self Portrait with Monkeys
Frida Kahlo



**Exploration of Abstract Forms:** Abstract artists like Wassily Kandinsky and Jackson Pollock pushed the boundaries of form and composition. Exploring abstract elements can add a dynamic and expressive quality to the design. A graphic designer shared, "Abstract art taught me to embrace ambiguity and let the viewer interpret the meaning. This can be incredibly powerful in design."

Black and Violet
Wassily Kandinsky

Image credits : www.wassilykandinsky.net

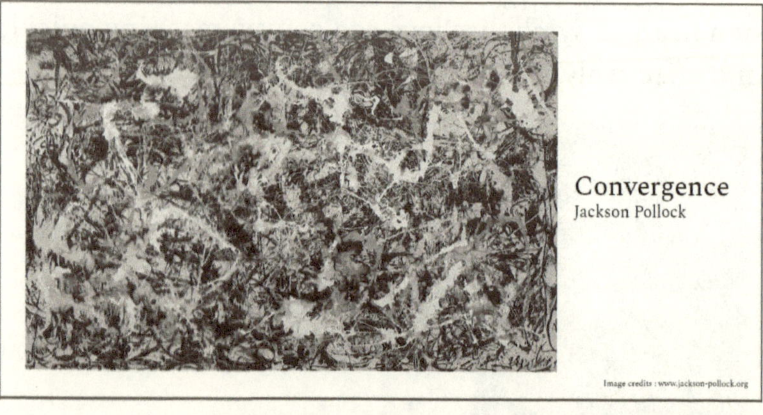

Convergence
Jackson Pollock

Image credits : www.jackson-pollock.org

**Innovation through Technique:** Artists like Leonardo da Vinci and Vincent van Gogh's innovative techniques demonstrate the importance of experimentation. Designers can benefit from experimenting with new tools and methods to create unique solutions. Da Vinci's anatomical sketches and Van Gogh's impasto technique show that pushing technical boundaries can lead to groundbreaking work.

The Vitruvian Man
Leonardo da Vinci

Image credits : www.leonardodavinci.net

The Starry Night
Vincent van Gogh

Image credits : By Vincent van Gogh -
bgEuwDxel93-Pg — Google Arts & Culture,

**Cultural Context and Relevance:** The works of artists like Diego Rivera and Yayoi Kusama reflect their cultural contexts and personal experiences. Understanding design projects' cultural and social context can lead to more relevant and meaningful solutions. A data artist on the podcast once said, "Design is not created in a vacuum. It's a reflection of the culture and time in which it exists."

Man at the Crossroads
Diego Rivera

Ascension of Polkadots
on the Trees
Yayoi Kusama



## Insights from Art: Case Studies

Exploring specific case studies where art and design intersect can provide deeper insights and inspiration:

### Case Study 1: The Bauhaus Movement

The Bauhaus movement, founded by Walter Gropius in 1919, sought to bridge the gap between art and industry by combining crafts and fine arts. Bauhaus artists and designers believed in integrating art, design, and technology to create functional and aesthetically pleasing objects. The movement's emphasis on simplicity, functionality, and the use of modern materials has had a lasting impact on both art and design. The iconic works of Bauhaus designers like Marcel Breuer and Wassily Kandinsky continue to influence contemporary design practices.

One of Bauhaus's key principles was that "form follows function," which has become a cornerstone of modern design. This principle encourages designers to prioritise usability and functionality without sacrificing aesthetics. The Bauhaus legacy reminds us that great design is both beautiful and practical.

### The Bauhaus Movement
Marcel Breuer

The Bauhaus is the most influential art and design school in history.
The image represents the Bauhaus 100 series, celebrating the centenary of the hugely influential design school.

Image credits : www.dezeen.com

## Case Study 2: Andy Warhol and Pop Art

Andy Warhol's work in the Pop Art movement blurred the lines between commercial art and fine art. By incorporating imagery from popular culture and mass media, Warhol challenged traditional notions of art and design. His use of repetition, bold colours, and commercial techniques like screen printing revolutionised the art world and influenced graphic design. Warhol's approach demonstrates the potential of combining artistic expression with commercial design principles to create impactful and accessible works.

Warhol's famous quote, "In the future, everyone will be world-famous for 15 minutes," reflects his understanding of the media's power and the fleeting nature of fame. His work teaches designers to embrace popular culture and use it as a source of inspiration, making their work more relatable and engaging.

Brillo Box
(Soap Pads)

Andy Warhol

Warhol's Brillo Box sculptures are life-size replicas of real shipping cartons by Brillo, a popular brand of American washing-up pads.

Image credits : Image © pedrosimoes7 /
Brillo Boxes© Andy Warhol 1964

## Case Study 3: Zaha Hadid and Architectural Design

Zaha Hadid, a pioneering architect known for her innovative and artistic approach to architecture, often blurred the lines between art and design. Her fluid and dynamic structures, such as the Guangzhou Opera House and the Heydar Aliyev Center, showcase her ability to integrate artistic principles into functional design. Hadid's work emphasises the importance of pushing creative boundaries and rethinking traditional design processes to achieve extraordinary results.

Hadid once said, "There are 360 degrees, so why stick to one?" This philosophy is evident in her designs, which often defy conventional geometric shapes and create new spatial experiences. Her work inspires designers to think beyond the ordinary and explore new forms and structures.

## Practical Applications: Integrating Art into Design

To effectively integrate artistic principles into design practice, consider the following strategies:

**Incorporate Artistic Techniques:** Experiment with artistic techniques such as painting, drawing, and sculpture to inspire new design ideas. These practices can help you explore different forms, textures, and compositions. For example, using hand-drawn sketches as a basis for digital designs can add a personal touch and unique character.

**Collaborate with Artists:** Seek opportunities to collaborate with artists on design projects. Their unique perspectives and skills can add depth and creativity to your work. A successful collaboration can result in a final product that is richer and more multifaceted than what either party could have achieved alone.

**Study Art History:** Regularly study art history to draw inspiration from various movements and artists. Analyse how they approached composition, colour, and form to inform your design decisions. Understanding artistic style's historical context and evolution can provide valuable insights into your design process.

**Create Art-Infused Designs:** Integrate artistic elements into your designs to create visually rich and engaging experiences. This can include using hand-drawn illustrations, abstract patterns, or expressive colour palettes. For example, incorporating elements of surrealism or cubism can add an intriguing and unexpected dimension to your work.

**Explore New Mediums:** Experiment with new mediums and materials inspired by art. This can lead to innovative design solutions and expand your creative horizons. For instance, using unconventional materials like recycled objects or digital media can create unique and sustainable designs.

## The Role of Design Studios in Blurring the Lines

Leading design studios worldwide have embraced the intersection of art and design, creating groundbreaking work that challenges traditional boundaries. Here are some examples:

## Studio Drift

Studio Drift, founded by Lonneke Gordijn and Ralph Nauta, combines art, design, and technology to create mesmerising installations and sculptures. Their work, such as the kinetic sculpture "Shylight" and the light installation "Franchise Freedom," explores the relationship between nature and technology. Studio Drift creates immersive experiences that captivate and inspire by integrating artistic concepts with cutting-edge technology. Their approach demonstrates how technology can be used to enhance creative expression, creating works that are both innovative and emotionally resonant. Studio Drift's work inspires designers to think beyond traditional mediums and explore the potential of technology to create new forms of art and design.

### Sagmeister & Walsh

Stefan Sagmeister and Jessica Walsh of Sagmeister & Walsh are known for their bold and artistic approach to graphic design. Their work often incorporates hand-crafted elements, experimental typography, and striking visuals. Projects like "Beauty," an exhibition exploring the concept of beauty in design, demonstrate their ability to merge art and design to create thought-provoking and visually stunning work.

Sagmeister & Walsh's emphasis on personal expression and experimentation encourages designers to take risks and push the boundaries of their creative practice. Their work shows that integrating artistic techniques into design can produce powerful and memorable visual experiences.

### Snarkitecture

Snarkitecture, founded by Daniel Arsham and Alex Mustonen, blurs the lines between art and architecture. Their projects, such as the interactive installation

"The Beach" and the retail space for KITH, transform everyday spaces into extraordinary experiences. By combining artistic expression with architectural design, Snarkitecture creates environments that challenge perceptions and engage the senses.

Their work highlights the potential of interdisciplinary collaboration to create immersive and interactive experiences. Snarkitecture's approach inspires designers to think about how their work can transform spaces and create meaningful interactions.

Snarkitecture
'The Beach' installation at the National Building Museum, Washington DC.



## Learning from Art: Personal Growth and Development

Studying and integrating art into your design practice can lead to personal growth and development. Here are some ways art can enrich your life and work:

**Cultivate Creativity:** Engaging with art stimulates creativity and encourages you to think outside the box. This can lead to more innovative and original design solutions. You can develop a unique creative voice by experimenting with different artistic techniques and styles.

**Enhance Observation Skills:** Art trains you to observe details and appreciate subtle nuances. These skills are valuable in design, where attention to detail can make a significant difference. For example, studying the brushwork in a painting can teach you to pay attention to the finer details in your designs.

**Develop Emotional Intelligence:** Art often explores emotions and human experiences. Engaging with art can help you develop empathy and emotional intelligence, which are crucial for creating user-centred designs. Understanding the emotional impact of your work can make it more meaningful and effective.

**Expand Cultural Awareness:** Studying art from different cultures and historical periods broadens your understanding of diverse perspectives. This awareness can inform your design work and make it more inclusive and relevant. You can create designs that resonate with a global audience by incorporating elements from different cultures.

**Foster Mindfulness and Reflection:** Creating and experiencing art can be a meditative practice that fosters mindfulness and self-reflection. This can lead to greater self-awareness and personal growth. Reflecting on your creative process and the meaning behind your work can deepen your understanding and enhance your practice.

## Conclusion: Embracing the Intersection of Art and Design

The intersection of art and design offers a rich and dynamic landscape for creativity and innovation. By incorporating artistic principles into design practice, embracing interdisciplinary collaboration, and learning from the rich history of art, designers can elevate their work to new heights. The fusion of art and design not only enhances the aesthetic quality of our work but also deepens its meaning and impact.

As designers, we can draw inspiration from the art world, integrate its principles into our practice, and create functional and beautiful work. By blurring the lines between art and design, we can create experiences that resonate deeply with users and stand the test of time.

# CHAPTER 11

## Designing for All: Creating Inclusive Experiences

Designing for accessibility is a moral and legal obligation and an opportunity to create inclusive and user-friendly experiences for everyone. Accessibility ensures that people with disabilities can access, understand, and interact with your designs. Here, we will explore the principles of accessible design, practical strategies for creating inclusive experiences, and the benefits of designing for accessibility.

### The Importance of Accessibility in Design

Accessibility is a fundamental aspect of good design. It ensures that products and services are usable by as many people as possible, regardless of their abilities. Here are key reasons why accessibility should be a priority:

**Legal and Ethical Responsibility:** Many countries have laws and regulations that require digital and physical environments to be accessible to people with disabilities.

Failing to follow these laws can cause legal consequences and damage your reputation.

**Broadening Your Audience:** By making your designs accessible, you reach a wider audience, including people with disabilities. This can increase user engagement, customer satisfaction, and market share.

**Enhancing User Experience:** Accessible design often leads to better usability for all users, not just those with disabilities. It encourages designers to think more carefully about user interactions, leading to more straightforward and intuitive interfaces.

**Promoting Inclusivity:** Accessibility is about creating equal opportunities for everyone. Designing inclusive experiences demonstrates your commitment to social responsibility and can enhance your brand's reputation.

**Innovation and Creativity:** Accessibility challenges designers to think outside the box and develop innovative solutions. This can lead to more creative and practical designs.

**Enhanced Brand Reputation:** Demonstrating a commitment to accessibility can enhance your brand's reputation and build trust with your audience. It shows that you value inclusivity and are dedicated to creating equal opportunities for everyone.

**Future-Proofing:** As technology and user expectations evolve, accessibility will continue to play a crucial role in design. By prioritising accessibility now, you ensure that your products and services remain relevant and usable in the future.

## Principles of Accessible Design

Accessible design is based on several fundamental principles that guide the creation of inclusive and user-friendly experiences:

**Perceivable**: Information and user interface components must be presented in ways that users can perceive. This includes providing text alternatives for non-text content, offering captions and transcripts for multimedia, and ensuring content is distinguishable from the background.

**Operable**: User interface components and navigation must be operable by all users. This includes making all functionality accessible via a keyboard, providing sufficient time for users to read and use content, and avoiding content that causes seizures.

**Understandable**: Information and the operation of the user interface must be understandable. This includes making text readable and understandable, ensuring that web pages appear and operate in predictable ways, and helping users avoid and correct mistakes.

**Robust**: Content must be strong enough to be interpreted reliably by various user agents, including assistive technologies. This includes using clean HTML code, ensuring compatibility with current and future technologies, and providing error messages that are easy to understand.

## Strategies for Creating Accessible Experiences

Creating inclusive experiences requires intentional effort and a commitment to accessibility throughout the design process. Here are some practical strategies to help you design for accessibility:

**Incorporate Accessibility from the Start:** Accessibility should be considered from the beginning of the design process. This includes user research, wireframing, prototyping, and testing. Incorporating accessibility early on can save time and resources compared to retrofitting existing designs.

**Understand Your Users:** Conduct research to understand the needs of users with disabilities, including people with visual, auditory, cognitive, and motor impairments. Engaging with users with disabilities through interviews, surveys, and usability testing can provide valuable insights and ensure your designs meet their needs.

**Use Semantic HTML:** Use semantic HTML to provide structure and meaning to your content. This helps screen readers and other assistive technologies interpret the content correctly. Use elements like headings, lists, and landmarks to create a clear and logical structure.

**Provide Text Alternatives:** Ensure that all non-text content, such as images, videos, and audio, has text alternatives. This includes alt text for images, video captions, and audio content transcripts. Text alternatives make content accessible to users with visual and hearing impairments.

**Ensure Keyboard Accessibility:** All interactive elements, such as buttons, links, and form controls, can be accessed and operated using a keyboard. This is crucial for users with motor impairments who rely on keyboard navigation.

**Design for Color Blindness:** Use colour combinations that are accessible to users with colour blindness. Avoid relying solely on colour to convey information and provide sufficient contrast between text and background colours. Tools like the WebAIM Color Contrast Checker can help you evaluate colour contrast.

**Provide Clear Instructions and Feedback:** Ensure your interface's instructions are clear and concise. Provide feedback on user actions, such as form submissions and errors. Use plain language and avoid jargon to make content more accessible and understandable.

**Test with Assistive Technologies:** Test your designs with various assistive technologies, such as screen readers, magnifiers, and voice recognition software. This can help you identify accessibility issues and ensure compatibility with different tools.

## Frameworks for Accessible Design

To help you integrate accessibility into your design process, here are some frameworks and guidelines to follow:

**Web Content Accessibility Guidelines (WCAG):** The WCAG, developed by the World Wide Web Consortium (W3C), provides comprehensive guidelines for making web content accessible. The guidelines are organised into four principles: Perceivable, Operable, Understandable, and Robust (POUR). Each principle includes testable success criteria and implementation techniques. The current version, WCAG 2.1, includes additional criteria for mobile accessibility.

**Inclusive Design Principles:** The Inclusive Design Principles provide guidelines for creating more accessible and inclusive user experiences. The principles emphasise designing for flexibility, simplicity, and clarity and encourage considering users' diverse needs.

**Universal Design:** Universal Design is a broader approach that aims to create products and environments usable by all people, to the greatest extent possible, without needing adaptation or specialised design. The principles of Universal Design include equitable use, flexibility in use, simple and intuitive use, perceptible information, tolerance for error, low physical effort, and size and space for approach and use.

## Real-Life Examples of Accessible Design

To illustrate the impact of accessible design, let's explore some examples of companies and products that have successfully integrated accessibility:

**Microsoft:** Microsoft is a leader in accessibility, continuously improving its products to make them more inclusive. The company's Office suite includes features like the Accessibility Checker, which helps users identify and fix accessibility issues in their documents.

Microsoft's Xbox Adaptive Controller is another example of inclusive design, providing customisable inputs for gamers with limited mobility.

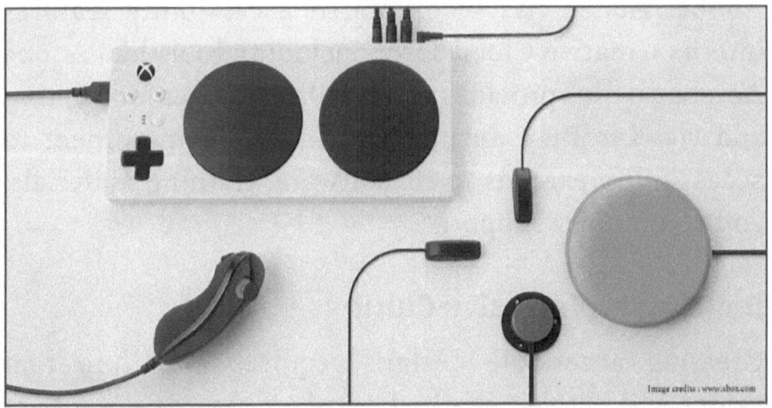


**Apple:** Apple has made significant strides in accessibility, integrating features like VoiceOver, a screen reader for iOS and macOS, and Switch Control, which allows users with motor impairments to control their devices using switches. Apple's commitment to accessibility has made its products more inclusive and user-friendly.

**Google:** Google has incorporated accessibility features across its products, including Chrome, Android, and Google Docs. Chrome includes extensions like ChromeVox, a screen reader, and high-contrast modes for users with visual impairments. Android's accessibility suite includes features like TalkBack, BrailleBack, and switch access.

**BBC:** The BBC has implemented accessibility best practices across its online platforms, ensuring that content is accessible to all users. The BBC's accessibility guidelines provide comprehensive recommendations for designing inclusive digital experiences, including techniques for making multimedia content accessible.

**Adobe:** Adobe has incorporated accessibility features into its Creative Cloud suite, including tools like Adobe Acrobat, which provides accessibility features for creating and viewing PDF documents. Adobe's commitment to accessibility extends to its software, training materials, and community support.

## Building an Inclusive Culture

Creating accessible designs requires a culture that values and actively works towards inclusivity. Here are some strategies to build an inclusive culture within your organisation:

**Educate and Train:** Provide training on accessibility best practices for all team members, including designers, developers, and content creators. Ensure everyone understands the importance of accessibility and how to implement it in their work.

**Set Clear Goals and Standards:** Establish clear accessibility goals and standards for your projects. Use frameworks like WCAG to guide your efforts and ensure consistency across your products and services.

**Integrate Accessibility into Processes:** Incorporate accessibility into your design and development processes. Include accessibility checks in your project timelines, conduct regular audits, and use tools like accessibility checkers to identify and fix issues.

**Foster Collaboration:** Encourage collaboration between designers, developers, and accessibility experts. Working together ensures that accessibility considerations are integrated throughout the project lifecycle.

**Listen to Feedback:** Actively seek feedback from users with disabilities. Use their insights to improve your designs and address any accessibility issues. This can help you create more inclusive and user-friendly experiences.

## Conclusion: Creating Inclusive Experiences

Designing for accessibility is not just about compliance—it's about creating inclusive experiences that empower all users. By incorporating accessibility into your design process, you ensure that your products and services are usable by everyone, regardless of their abilities.

Embrace the principles of accessible design, utilise frameworks and guidelines, and continuously test and refine your designs to ensure inclusivity. Remember that accessibility is an ongoing journey that requires commitment and dedication.

Your efforts to create accessible experiences will benefit users with disabilities and enhance your designs' overall usability and appeal. By prioritising accessibility, you contribute to a more inclusive and equitable world where everyone can access and enjoy the products and services you create.

# CHAPTER 12

## Designing Beyond Screens: Expanding Horizons

Design is not limited to pixels on our screens. The world around us offers vast opportunities for creativity and innovation beyond the digital realm. This chapter explores the principles and practices of designing physical products, spatial experiences, and environmentally responsible designs. Expanding our horizons can create holistic experiences that enrich people's lives in tangible ways.

### The Evolution of Design: From Digital to Physical

The principles of good design extend far beyond the confines of our screens. As technology advances, the lines between digital and physical design are increasingly blurred, creating new opportunities for designers to innovate in the physical world.

One of the podcast guests, an expert in industrial design, aptly noted, "Design is about solving problems and creating meaningful experiences, whether on a screen or in the real world. The same principles apply, but the context and medium change."

## Designing Physical Products

Designing physical products requires a deep understanding of materials, manufacturing processes, and user interactions. Here are some fundamental principles for designing physical products:

### Functionality and Usability

Just like digital interfaces, physical products must be functional and user-friendly. The design should prioritise ease of use and intuitive interactions. For instance, consider how ergonomics play a crucial role in product design, ensuring that products are comfortable and efficient to use.

One designer shared, "When we designed a new kitchen appliance, we spent months observing how people use their kitchens, noting every motion and touchpoint. The result was a product that felt intuitive from the first use."

Functionality is more than just basic usability. It includes considering how other users will use the product in different contexts,, and under various conditions. For example, a well-designed kitchen knife should be balanced, comfortable to hold for extended periods, and sharp enough to cut through a variety of foods with minimal effort.

## Aesthetics and Form

A product's visual appeal is essential for creating an emotional connection with users. The form, colour, texture, and overall aesthetics should align with the product's purpose and brand identity. As one designer shared, "A well-designed product is a joy to look at and to use."

Take, for example, the classic Eames Lounge Chair. Its sleek, inviting form and luxurious materials make it not just a piece of furniture but an experience. Its design communicates comfort and sophistication, inviting users to engage with it.

Aesthetics go beyond mere appearance. They encompass the emotional response that a product elicits. A beautifully designed product can evoke joy, satisfaction, and pride in ownership. It can also enhance the user experience by making the product more enjoyable.

## Material Selection

The choice of materials affects a product's aesthetics, durability, and environmental impact. Designers should consider sustainable materials and eco-friendly manufacturing processes. Using recycled or biodegradable materials can significantly reduce a product's environmental footprint.

A design leader mentioned, "We started using bamboo for its sustainability and strength. It reduced our carbon footprint and gave our products a unique, natural look that resonated with our customers."

Material selection also involves understanding the properties of different materials and how they can be manipulated to achieve the desired form and function. For example, metals can be polished for a sleek finish, plastics can be moulded into complex shapes, and fabrics can add texture and warmth.

## Prototyping and Testing

Prototyping is a critical step in the design process. Creating physical prototypes allows designers to test functionality, ergonomics, and user interactions. Iterative testing and refinement are crucial for developing successful products. A product designer once mentioned, "Prototyping is where ideas come to life. It's where we see what works and what doesn't."

Dyson is renowned for its rigorous prototyping process. They tested over 5,000 prototypes before finalising their first bagless vacuum cleaner, ensuring perfect detail.

Prototyping can take many forms, from simple cardboard mockups to fully functional 3D-printed models. Each iteration provides valuable insights that can be used to refine the design. Testing with real users is especially important, as it can reveal issues that designers might not have anticipated.

## Human-Centred Design

Understanding users' needs and behaviours is fundamental. Human-centred design ensures that the product meets the needs of its intended users and enhances their experiences. This involves conducting user research, gathering feedback, and continuously iterating on the design.

A guest from the podcast emphasised, "We need to remember that every product we design is for someone to use. Putting ourselves in their shoes and understanding their context is key to creating something beneficial."

Human-centred design is about empathy. It requires designers to deeply understand the people they are designing for, including their goals, challenges, and preferences. Techniques such as personas, user journey mapping, and usability testing can provide valuable insights into user needs and behaviours.

## Designing Spatial Experiences

Designing spatial experiences involves creating functional, aesthetically pleasing, and emotionally engaging environments. Here are some fundamental principles for designing spatial experiences:

### Functionality and Flow

The layout and organisation of a space should facilitate easy movement and access. Flow should be intuitive and efficient when designing a retail store, office, or public space. Consider how the furniture, pathways, and signage arrangement can guide users through the space.

In designing a new workspace for a tech company, a designer noted, "We mapped out every employee's daily journey to ensure they had everything they needed within easy reach, from coffee stations to meeting rooms."

Functionality in spatial design also includes considering the specific activities that will take place in the space and ensuring that the layout supports these activities. For example, a well-designed kitchen should have a logical arrangement of appliances and work surfaces to facilitate cooking.

## Aesthetics and Atmosphere

The visual and sensory elements of a space significantly impact the user experience. Lighting, colour schemes, textures, and decor all contribute to the atmosphere. A well-designed space should evoke the desired emotions and complement its intended use. For example, a spa might use soft lighting, soothing colours, and natural materials to create a relaxing environment.

An architect shared, "In our design for a boutique hotel, we used warm woods, lush fabrics, and subtle lighting to create an atmosphere of understated luxury and comfort."

Aesthetics in spatial design also involves creating a sense of place and identity. This can be achieved through thoughtful use of materials, colours, and forms that reflect the culture and history of the location. For example, incorporating local materials and craftsmanship can give a space a unique character and sense of authenticity.

## User-Centred Design

Like physical products, understanding users' needs and preferences is crucial. Conducting user research and gathering feedback can inform the design of functional and enjoyable spaces. One architect mentioned, "Designing a space is about creating an experience. It's about how people feel and interact within that environment."

For instance, extensive research with patients, families, and staff informed every aspect of designing a children's hospital, from the layout of patient rooms to the colour schemes used in common areas, ensuring a healing and comforting environment.

User-centred design in spatial experiences involves considering the users' physical, cognitive, and emotional needs. This can include designing for accessibility, creating intuitive wayfinding systems, and incorporating elements that promote well-being and comfort.

## Sustainability

Sustainable design practices are essential for creating environmentally responsible spaces. This includes using eco-friendly materials and energy-efficient systems and designing for long-term use and adaptability. Incorporating green roofs, solar panels, and natural ventilation can enhance a building's sustainability.

A sustainable architect noted, "Every building we design has to stand the test of time. We choose materials that age well and systems that reduce energy consumption over the building's lifecycle."

Sustainability in spatial design also involves considering the environmental impact of the construction process and the building's operation. This can include minimising waste during construction, designing for energy efficiency, and using renewable energy sources.

## Flexibility and Adaptability

Spaces should be designed flexibly to accommodate changing needs and functions. Modular furniture, movable partitions, and adaptable layouts can make spaces more versatile. This is especially important in dynamic environments like offices and event spaces.

A workspace designer shared, "We created a flexible office layout with movable walls and multi-functional furniture, allowing the space to be reconfigured for different uses, from team meetings to large events."

Flexibility in spatial design also includes designing for future growth and change. This can involve creating adaptable systems and infrastructure that can easily be modified or expanded as needs evolve.

## Environmentally Responsible Design

Environmental responsibility is a critical consideration in modern design. As designers, we are responsible for minimising our work's environmental impact. Here are some principles for environmentally responsible design:

### Sustainable Materials

Choosing sustainable materials reduces a product or space's environmental footprint. This includes using recycled, recyclable, or biodegradable materials. As an artist shared in our conversation, "Sustainability is about making choices that are good for the planet and future generations."

One company has pioneered the use of ocean plastic in their products, turning waste into high-quality materials for everything from shoes to furniture, demonstrating a commitment to environmental sustainability.

Sustainable materials also include those sourced responsibly, such as FSC-certified wood, which ensures that the wood comes from sustainably managed forests. Designers should also consider the entire lifecycle of the materials, from extraction to disposal.

### Energy Efficiency

Designing for energy efficiency helps reduce the environmental impact of buildings and products. This includes using energy-efficient systems, renewable energy sources, and designing for passive heating and cooling. Incorporating features like LED lighting, energy-efficient appliances, and smart thermostats can significantly reduce energy consumption.

An environmental engineer mentioned, "Our new office building uses a combination of solar panels and smart energy management systems, reducing our energy consumption by 40% compared to traditional buildings."

Energy efficiency in design also includes considering the orientation and layout of buildings to maximise natural light and ventilation, reducing the need for artificial lighting and air conditioning. Designing for passive solar heating and cooling can further enhance energy efficiency.

## Life Cycle Thinking

Considering a product or space's entire life cycle, from production to disposal, is essential. This involves designing for durability, repairability, and recyclability. By considering a product's end of life, designers can create solutions that minimise waste and promote circularity.

In the podcast, a designer shared about a furniture concept he was working on: "We design our furniture to be easily disassembled, allowing parts to be replaced or recycled, extending the product's lifespan and reducing waste."

Lifecycle thinking also involves considering the environmental impact of the production process, including the use of resources and the generation of waste. By designing for minimal resource use and waste generation, designers can reduce the overall environmental footprint of their products and spaces.

## Waste Reduction

Reducing waste in the design and manufacturing process is crucial. This includes designing for minimal material use, reusing and recycling materials, and reducing packaging waste. For example, designing flat-pack furniture that minimises material waste and shipping volume can significantly reduce environmental impact.

A packaging designer noted, "We redesigned our packaging to use 50% less material and made it fully recyclable, which benefits the environment and reduces shipping costs."

Waste reduction also involves designing for reuse and repurposing. This can include creating products that can be easily disassembled and reassembled or designing spaces that can be easily modified and adapted for different uses.

## Biophilic Design

Incorporating natural elements into design can enhance well-being and reduce environmental impact. This includes using natural materials, incorporating greenery, and designing for natural light and ventilation. Biophilic design principles can create spaces that promote health and well-being while connecting people with nature.

An interior designer shared, "In our latest project, we integrated indoor gardens and large windows to bring in natural light, creating a vibrant and alive space that enhances the occupants' well-being."

Biophilic design also involves creating environments that mimic natural ecosystems, promoting a sense of harmony and balance. This can include incorporating water features, natural ventilation, and views of nature, all of which have been shown to improve mental and physical health.

## Inspiring Examples of Designing Beyond Screens

To understand the impact of designing beyond screens, let's explore some inspiring examples from leading designers and studios around the world:

### Dyson: Innovating Physical Products

Dyson, founded by Sir James Dyson, is known for its innovative approach to physical product design. Dyson's products are characterised by their functionality, aesthetics, and cutting-edge technology, from vacuum cleaners to bladeless fans. Dyson's design philosophy emphasises problem-solving and engineering excellence, resulting in products that perform exceptionally and look sleek and modern.

One of Dyson's iconic products, the Dyson Airblade hand dryer, exemplifies this approach. By rethinking the traditional hand dryer, Dyson created a faster, more hygienic, and more energy-efficient product. The Airblade's innovative design has set a new standard in its category and demonstrates the power of combining engineering and design.

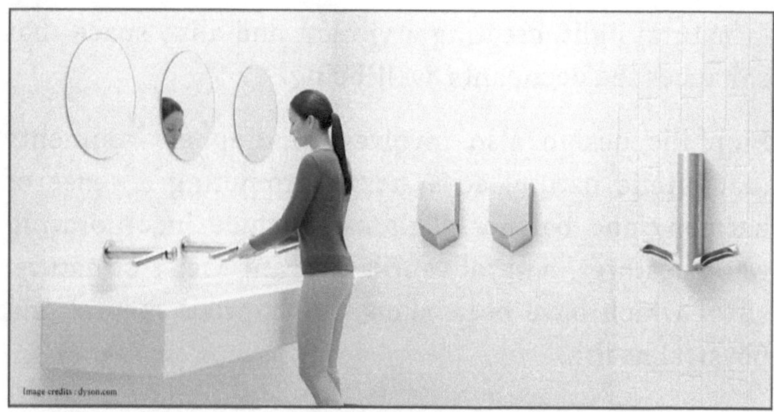



Dyson's iterative prototyping process is key to their success. They extensively test each design iteration, ensuring the final product meets high performance and durability standards. This commitment to excellence is evident in their products, which consistently deliver innovative solutions to everyday problems.

## IKEA: Designing for Sustainability

IKEA is a global leader in sustainable design, offering affordable, stylish, and eco-friendly products. IKEA's commitment to sustainability is evident in its use of sustainable materials, energy-efficient production processes, and innovative recycling programs. The company's flat-pack furniture design minimises material use and reduces shipping volume, contributing to lower carbon emissions.

Image credits : logisticsmgepsupv.wordpress.com

IKEA's approach to design extends beyond products to include the design of its stores and supply chain. The company's commitment to sustainability is reflected in initiatives like the IKEA Circular Hub, which promotes the reuse and recycling of furniture, and the introduction of solar panels and energy-efficient lighting in its stores.

IKEA's philosophy of "democratic design" emphasises the balance of form, function, quality, sustainability, and low price. This holistic approach ensures their products are accessible, environmentally friendly, and aesthetically pleasing, making sustainable design achievable for a broad audience.

**MASS Design Group: Human-Centred Spaces**

MASS Design Group, a non-profit architecture firm, designs spaces that promote health, well-being, and social justice. Their work includes hospitals, schools, and community centres designed to meet the needs of their users and the surrounding communities. MASS Design

Group emphasises participatory design, sustainability, and local materials and labour use.

One notable project is Butaro District Hospital, Rwanda. Designed in collaboration with local communities and healthcare professionals, the hospital features natural ventilation, abundant natural light, and outdoor spaces that promote healing. The project demonstrates how thoughtful design can profoundly impact health and well-being.

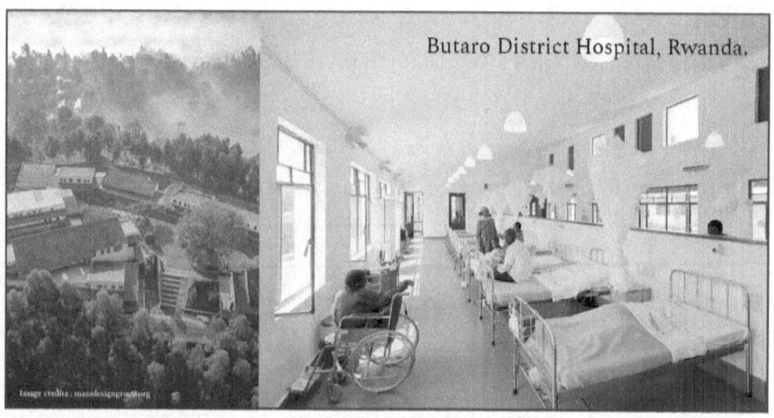


MASS Design Group's participatory approach ensures that its designs are deeply rooted in the needs and aspirations of the communities it serves. By involving local stakeholders in the design process, it creates functional, beautiful, culturally, and socially relevant spaces.

## Practical Applications: Expanding Horizons

To effectively design beyond screens, consider the following strategies:

## Embrace Interdisciplinary Collaboration

Collaborate with experts in fields such as industrial design, architecture, and environmental science. Their insights can inform and enhance your design work. For example, working with an environmental engineer can help you incorporate sustainable practices into your designs.

An example of successful interdisciplinary collaboration is the development of sustainable packaging solutions that combine design aesthetics with environmental science to create eco-friendly and visually appealing products.

## Conduct User Research

Understanding users' needs and behaviours is crucial for designing effective physical products and spaces. Conduct user research, gather feedback, and iterate your designs using real-world insights. This human-centred approach ensures that your designs are both functional and user-friendly.

In designing a new public park, extensive community engagement and feedback sessions ensured that the final design met the needs and desires of local residents, resulting in a well-used and beloved space.

## Experiment with Materials and Technologies

Stay informed about new materials and technologies that can enhance your designs. Experiment with sustainable materials, smart technologies, and innovative manufacturing processes. For example, exploring biodegradable plastics or 3D printing can open up new possibilities for product design.

A designer shared, "We started experimenting with 3D-printed ceramics, which allowed us to create intricate designs previously impossible with traditional methods."

## Focus on Sustainability

Prioritise sustainability in your design practice. Choose eco-friendly materials, design for energy efficiency, and consider the entire life cycle of your products and spaces. Incorporating sustainability into your designs benefits the environment and resonates with increasingly eco-conscious consumers.

In designing a new office building, sustainable practices such as using reclaimed wood, installing solar panels, and incorporating rainwater harvesting systems were implemented, significantly reducing the building's environmental impact.

## Create Holistic Experiences

Design with the entire user experience in mind, considering how digital and physical elements can work together seamlessly. For example, integrating digital interfaces with physical products can create more intuitive and engaging user experiences.

An example is a smart home system that seamlessly integrates physical devices with a user-friendly app, allowing users to control lighting, temperature, and security from their smartphones.

## Conclusion: Expanding Horizons

Designing beyond screens offers many opportunities to create meaningful and impactful experiences in the physical world. By applying the principles of good design to physical products, spatial experiences, and environmentally responsible designs, we can expand our horizons and make a positive difference in people's lives.

As designers, we can transform the physical world, making it more functional, beautiful, and sustainable. By embracing the challenges and opportunities of designing beyond screens, we can create holistic experiences that enrich the lives of our users and contribute to a more sustainable future.

Embrace the principles of good design, collaborate with experts, and let your creativity soar as you explore the limitless possibilities beyond the digital realm.

By focusing on functionality, aesthetics, sustainability, and user-centred design, we can create products and spaces that profoundly enhance people's lives. As we continue to push the boundaries of what design can achieve, let's remember the importance of empathy, collaboration, and innovation in our journey to create a better world.

# CHAPTER 13

## The Art and Science of Data-Driven Design

Data is a powerful tool that can transform the design process, providing invaluable insights and guiding decisions to create more effective and user-centred designs. Integrating data into your design process allows you to uncover patterns, understand user behaviours, and validate design choices. This chapter dives into the art and science of data-driven design, exploring how to seamlessly integrate data, create impactful visualisations, leverage data for deeper insights, and use data to grow your career and enhance design leadership.

### The Role of Data in Design

Data helps at every stage of the design process, from initial research and ideation to prototyping and testing. It provides a solid foundation for making informed decisions and helps ensure that designs meet users' needs and preferences.

One of the guests on my podcast, an expert in UX research, shared, "Data is not just numbers; it's the voice of the users. It tells us their needs, frustrations, and behaviours. By listening to this voice, we can create designs that truly resonate with them."

**Integrating Data into the Design Process**

To effectively integrate data into your design process, consider the following steps:

**Define Your Goals and Metrics:** Start by clearly defining what you want to achieve and the metrics that will help you measure success. This could include user engagement, task completion rates, or conversion rates. Clear goals and metrics ensure that you collect relevant data and focus your efforts on what matters most.

**Collect Data:** Use various methods to collect data, including user surveys, interviews, analytics tools, and usability tests. Each method provides different insights and helps comprehensively understand user needs and behaviours. Combining quantitative data (such as click-through rates and time on page) with qualitative data (such as user feedback and interviews) gives a fuller picture.

**Analyse and Interpret Data:** Once you've collected the data, analyse it to uncover patterns, trends, and insights. Use statistical methods and data visualisation tools to make sense of the data and identify key findings. Look for correlations, anomalies, and user behaviours that can inform your design decisions.

**Incorporate Data into Design:** Use the insights gained from data analysis to inform your design decisions. This could involve changing a design's layout, functionality, or aesthetics based on user feedback and behavioural data. Continuously iterate on your designs, using data to validate and refine them.

**Test and Validate:** After making data-informed design changes, test the updated design with users to validate its effectiveness. Use A/B testing, usability testing, and other methods to gather feedback and measure the impact of the changes. This iterative process ensures that your designs continuously improve and align with user needs.

## Creating Impactful Data Visualisations

Data visualisation is an essential skill for designers, enabling them to communicate complex information clearly and effectively. Here are some principles for creating impactful data visualisations:

**Know Your Audience:** Understand who will view the data visualisation and what they need to know. Tailor the visualisation to their level of expertise and the key messages you want to convey. For example, a visualisation for a technical audience may include more detailed data and technical terms, while one for a general audience should focus on clarity and simplicity.

**Choose the Right Type of Visualization:** Different data visualisations are suited to different data types and messages. Common types include bar charts, line graphs, pie charts, scatter plots, and heat maps. Choose the type that best represents the data and highlights the key insights.

**Simplify and Focus:** Avoid cluttering the visualisation with too much information. Focus on the critical data points and insights, and use visual elements such as colour, size, and position to draw attention to them. Simplifying the visualisation helps ensure that the key messages are easily understood.

**Use Colour Effectively:** Colour can enhance the readability and impact data visualisation. Use colour to highlight important data points, differentiate between categories, and convey meaning. Be mindful of colour blindness and ensure the visualisation remains clear and accessible to all viewers.

**Provide Context:** Include labels, legends, and explanations to provide context and help viewers understand the data. Annotations can highlight key insights and guide the viewer through the visualisation. Providing context ensures viewers can interpret the data accurately and draw meaningful conclusions.

**Tell a Story:** Use data visualisation to tell a compelling story. Structure the visualisation to guide the viewer through the data, highlighting the key insights and their implications. A well-told data story can make the information more engaging and memorable.

## Leveraging Data for Deeper Insights

Data-driven design goes beyond simply collecting and analysing data; it involves using data to gain deeper insights and drive meaningful improvements. Here are some strategies for leveraging data to enhance your design process:

**Identify User Pain Points:** Use data to identify common user pain points and areas of friction in the user experience. This could include high drop-off rates, frequent error messages, or low engagement with specific features. Addressing these pain points can improve the overall user experience and increase satisfaction.

**Understand User Journeys:** Map out user journeys and identify critical touch points where users interact with your design. Use data to understand how users move through these touchpoints, where they encounter obstacles, and what actions they take. This holistic view helps you design more seamless and intuitive user experiences.

**Personalise Experiences:** Leverage data to create personalised user experiences. This could involve using user preferences, behaviours, and demographics to tailor content, recommendations, and interactions. Personalisation can enhance user engagement and make the experience more relevant and enjoyable.

**Predict Future Behaviour:** Use predictive analytics to forecast user behaviours and trends. This can help you anticipate user needs, identify emerging patterns, and make proactive design decisions. For example, predicting a spike in user traffic can help you optimise the design to handle increased load and ensure a smooth user experience.

**Benchmark and Compare:** Use data to benchmark your design against industry standards and competitors. Identify areas where your design excels and areas where it falls short. This comparative analysis can provide valuable insights and guide your efforts to improve and innovate.

**Measure Impact and ROI:** Track key metrics to measure the impact of your design changes and calculate the return on investment (ROI). This could include user satisfaction, engagement, conversion rates, and revenue. Measuring impact helps you understand the effectiveness of your design and justify future investments.

## Using Data to Grow in Your Career

Data is a tool for improving design and a valuable asset for personal and professional growth. By harnessing the power of data, you can enhance your skills, demonstrate your value, and advance your career.

**Build a Data-Backed Portfolio:** Showcase your ability to use data to inform design decisions in your portfolio. Include case studies highlighting how you collected, analysed, and applied data to create compelling designs. Demonstrating your data-driven approach can set you apart from other candidates and show potential employers that you make informed, impactful decisions.

**Develop Analytical Skills:** Invest in developing your data analysis skills. Learn to use tools like Google Analytics, Tableau, and Excel to collect and analyse data. Understanding statistical methods and being able to interpret data will make you a more effective designer and a valuable asset to any team.

**Stay Informed:** Keep up with the latest trends and best practices in data-driven design. Follow industry blogs, attend conferences, and participate in webinars to stay informed about new tools, techniques, and case studies. Staying current with industry developments will help you continuously improve your skills and remain competitive.

**Seek Feedback and Iterate:** Use data to gather feedback on your work and identify areas for improvement. Continuously iterate on your designs based on user feedback and data insights. Demonstrating a commitment to continuous improvement and data-driven decision-making will show employers and clients that you are dedicated to delivering the best possible outcomes.

**Leverage Data for Career Decisions:** Use data to inform your career decisions. Research industry trends, salary benchmarks, and job market demands to make informed choices about your career path. Understanding the data can help you identify growth opportunities, negotiate better compensation, and make strategic career moves.

**Design Leadership: Using Data to Drive Decisions**

As a design leader, using data to drive decisions is essential for creating a high-performing design team and delivering impactful results. Here are some strategies for integrating data into design leadership:

**Set Clear Goals and Metrics:** Define clear goals and metrics for your design team. Use data to track progress and measure success. Having clear metrics helps ensure that the team stays focused on what matters most and can measure the impact of their work.

**Foster a Data-Driven Culture:** Promote a culture of data-driven decision-making within your team. Encourage team members to use data to inform their design choices and validate their assumptions. Provide training and resources to help your team develop data literacy and analytical skills.

**Use Data for Performance Management:** Use data to assess team performance and identify areas for improvement. Track metrics such as project timelines, quality of work, and user satisfaction to evaluate individual and team performance. Use this data to provide constructive feedback and support professional development.

**Inform Strategic Decisions:** Use data to inform strategic decisions about design direction, resource allocation, and project prioritisation. Analysing data can help you identify trends, forecast future needs, and make informed decisions that align with business goals.

**Communicate with Stakeholders:** Use data to communicate the value and impact of design to stakeholders. Create compelling data visualisations and reports highlighting key insights, successes, and areas for improvement. Using data to tell a story can help build trust and buy-in from stakeholders.

**Invest in Data Tools and Technologies:** Ensure your team has access to the tools and technologies needed to collect, analyse, and visualise data. Investing in the right tools can enhance the team's ability to make data-driven decisions and deliver high-quality designs.

## Case Studies in Data-Driven Design Leadership

To illustrate the power of data-driven design leadership, let's explore some inspiring case studies from leading companies and designers:

### Case Study 1: IBM

IBM is renowned for its data-driven approach to design and innovation. The company's Enterprise Design Thinking framework integrates data into every stage of the design process, from research and ideation to testing and validation. IBM uses data to inform design decisions, track project progress, and measure the impact of design changes.

One notable example is IBM's use of data to optimise the user experience of its Watson platform. By analysing user interactions and feedback, the design team identified key pain points and areas for improvement. Data-driven design changes resulted in a more intuitive and user-friendly interface, enhancing user satisfaction and engagement.

### Case Study 2: Netflix

Netflix uses data to drive design and content decisions. The company uses data to understand user preferences, provide personalised recommendations, and optimise the user interface. By analysing viewing habits, Netflix can predict what content will resonate with different user segments and tailor the user experience accordingly.

Netflix's data-driven approach extends to its A/B testing framework. The company continuously tests design variations to determine what works best for its users. This iterative process ensures that Netflix's design decisions are based on empirical evidence, leading to a more engaging and practical user experience.

### Case Study 3: Google

Google is a pioneer in data-driven design and decision-making. The company uses data to inform every aspect of its design process, from user research and prototyping to testing and validation. Its extensive A/B testing exemplifies Google's data-driven culture to optimise product features and user interfaces.

One example is Google's redesign of its search results page. By analysing user data and conducting A/B tests, the design team identified opportunities to enhance the clarity and usability of search results. Data-driven design changes led to a cleaner, more intuitive interface that improved user satisfaction and search efficiency.

## Frameworks for Data-Driven Design

To fully leverage data in your design process, consider adopting the following frameworks:

### The Double Diamond Model

The Double Diamond model, developed by the Design Council, is a visual representation of the design process divided into four phases: Discover, Define, Develop, and Deliver. Integrating data into each phase can enhance the effectiveness of this model:

# Double Diamond Model

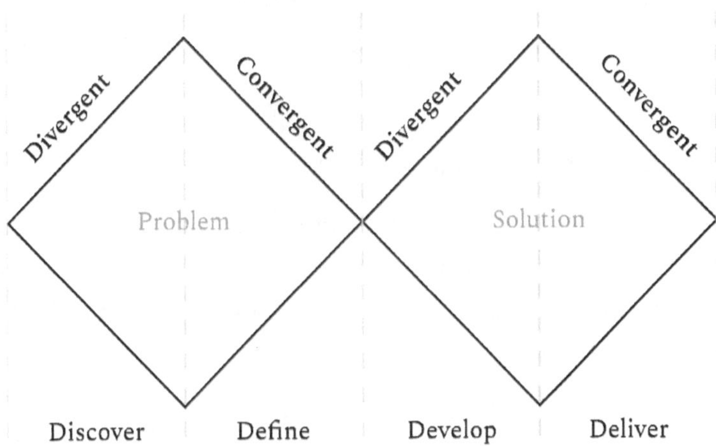



**Discover:** Use data to gather insights about user needs, behaviours, and pain points. Conduct surveys, interviews, and usability tests to collect qualitative and quantitative data. This phase is about exploring the problem space and understanding the context.

**Define:** Analyse the collected data to identify key themes and insights. Use this information to define the problem statement and design goals. This phase involves synthesising the data to create a clear and actionable design brief.

**Develop:** Based on the defined problem and goals, generate ideas and create prototypes. Use data to inform design decisions and validate concepts through user testing and feedback. This phase focuses on iterative development and refinement.

**Deliver:** Implement the final design and continuously monitor its performance using data. Use analytics tools to track key metrics and gather ongoing feedback. This phase ensures the design meets user needs and achieves the desired outcomes.

## The Lean UX Framework

The Lean UX framework emphasises rapid experimentation, continuous learning, and iterative design. Integrating data into this framework can enhance its effectiveness:

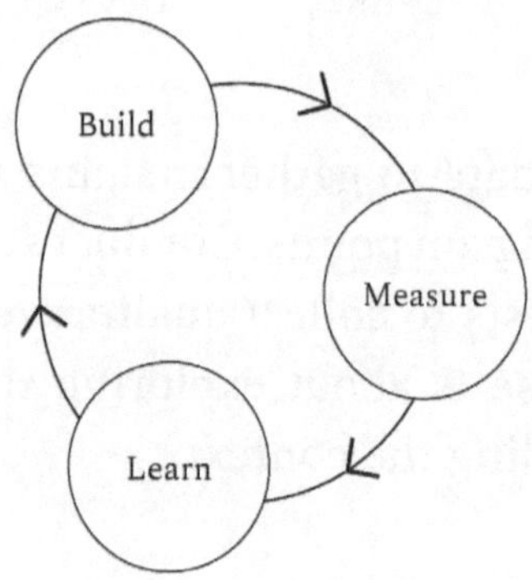

The Lean UX Framework

**Build:** Create minimal viable products (MVPs) or prototypes to test key hypotheses. Use data to identify critical assumptions and prioritise design efforts. This phase involves creating and deploying testable solutions quickly.

**Measure:** Collect data to evaluate MVP or prototype performance. Use analytics tools, user feedback, and usability tests to gather insights. This phase focuses on measuring the impact of design changes and validating assumptions.

**Learn:** Analyse the collected data to draw insights and refine the design. Use this information to iterate the design and make informed decisions. This phase emphasises continuous learning and improvement.

## Practical Applications: Embracing Data-Driven Design

To fully embrace data-driven design, consider the following practical applications:

### Establish a Data-Driven Culture

Promote a culture of data-driven decision-making within your organisation. Encourage team members to use data to inform their design choices and validate their assumptions. Provide training and resources to help your team develop data literacy and analytical skills.

A design lead shared, "Creating a data-driven culture starts with leadership. When leaders prioritise data and make it a core part of the design process, it sets the tone for the entire team."

## Invest in Data Tools and Technologies

Invest in tools and technologies that enable data collection, analysis, and visualisation. This could include analytics platforms, user testing tools, and data visualisation software. Ensure your team has access to the tools they need to gather and interpret data effectively.

Examples of popular data tools include Google Analytics, Hotjar, and Tableau. These tools provide valuable insights into user behaviours, preferences, and interactions, helping designers make informed decisions.

## Collaborate with Data Experts

Collaborate with data analysts, data scientists, and other experts to enhance your data-driven design efforts. These professionals can provide valuable insights, help interpret complex data, and guide you in making data-informed decisions.

One designer mentioned, "Working with data scientists has transformed our design process. Their expertise in analysing and interpreting data has helped us uncover deeper insights and create more effective designs."

## Continuously Iterate and Improve

Data-driven design is an iterative process. Continuously collect and analyse data to refine and improve your designs. Use A/B testing, usability testing, and other methods to validate design changes and measure their impact.

A product leader shared, "We never stop iterating on our designs. Data helps us see what's working and what's not, so we can continuously improve and deliver a better user experience."

## Conclusion: The Art and Science of Data-Driven Design

Data-driven design combines the art of creativity with the science of data analysis. You can create beautiful and practical designs by integrating data into your design process, creating impactful visualisations, and leveraging data for deeper insights.

Embrace the power of data to inform your decisions, validate your assumptions, and drive meaningful improvements. Adopting a data-driven approach ensures that your designs meet your users' needs, deliver impactful experiences, and achieve your business goals.

# CHAPTER 14

## AI and the Creative Process: A New Frontier

Artificial Intelligence (AI) is revolutionising the design industry, inaugurating a new era where creativity and technology intersect to produce extraordinary results. This chapter explores how AI can enhance creativity, the ethical considerations it brings, and practical applications in design. We will dive into the latest AI models, provide examples of their impact, and discuss how designers can leverage AI to design and scale products. Additionally, we will explore the fascinating world of generative art, where AI is used to create unique and compelling works of art. We will also address common concerns about AI replacing human jobs and how AI can be a powerful enabler for designers.

### The Role of AI in Enhancing Creativity

AI has the potential to augment human creativity by providing new tools and capabilities that were previously unimaginable. By automating routine tasks, generating new ideas, and offering insights based on vast amounts of data, AI can free designers to focus on more strategic and creative aspects of their work.

One of the guests on my podcast, an AI expert in design, shared, "AI is like a collaborator that can offer fresh perspectives and augment our creative abilities. It's not about replacing designers but empowering them to achieve more."

## Latest AI Models in Design

Several cutting-edge AI models are transforming the design landscape. Here are some of the most influential:

**Generative Adversarial Networks (GANs):** GANs consist of two neural networks—a generator and a discriminator—that work together to create realistic images, designs, and even art. They are used in fashion design, product design, and visual content creation. For example, NVIDIA's GauGAN can transform simple sketches into photorealistic images, enabling designers to visualise concepts quickly.

**Deep Learning Models:** Models like OpenAI's GPT-4 and DALL-E can generate text and images based on user inputs. GPT-4 can assist in generating design briefs, writing content, and brainstorming ideas, while DALL-E can create unique images from textual descriptions. These tools can inspire designers and help them explore new creative directions.

**Reinforcement Learning:** This type of AI learns by interacting with its environment and receiving feedback. In design, reinforcement learning can optimise layouts, workflows, and user interfaces by continuously improving based on user interactions. Google DeepMind's AlphaGo, which mastered the game of Go, exemplifies the power of reinforcement learning, showing its potential in solving complex design problems.

**Neural Style Transfer:** This AI technique allows designers to apply the artistic style of one image to another. It can be used in graphic design, photography, and video production to create visually stunning effects. Tools like Prisma and DeepArt use neural style transfer to transform photos into artworks in various styles.

## Practical Applications of AI in Design

AI offers numerous practical applications in design, enhancing creativity and efficiency. Here are some ways AI is being used in the industry:

**Automating Routine Tasks:** AI can automate repetitive tasks such as resizing images, creating templates, and generating design variations. This allows designers to focus on more complex and creative aspects of their work. Tools like Adobe Sensei use AI to automate mundane tasks, improving productivity and consistency.

**Generating Ideas and Concepts:** AI can help generate new ideas and concepts by analysing existing designs and creating variations. This can be particularly useful in the early stages of the design process when exploring different directions. For example, Autodesk's Dreamcatcher generates multiple design alternatives based on specified constraints and objectives, offering designers a range of innovative solutions.

**Personalising User Experiences**: AI can analyse user data to create personalised design experiences. This includes tailoring content, layouts, and interactions to individual preferences. Netflix uses AI to personalise its user interface, recommending content based on viewing habits and preferences, resulting in a more engaging and user-centric experience.

**Optimising Design Decisions**: AI can provide insights and recommendations to optimise design decisions. AI can suggest improvements and enhancements by analysing data on user behaviour, preferences, and performance metrics. Shopify's Kit uses AI to help e-commerce businesses optimise their online stores, recommending design changes to increase conversions and sales.

**Enhancing Creativity**: AI can augment human creativity by offering new tools and capabilities. For example, AI-powered tools like Runway ML allow designers to experiment with machine learning models to create unique visuals, animations, and interactive experiences. These tools open up new creative possibilities and push the boundaries of traditional design.

## Generative Art: Blurring the Lines Between Art and Design

**Generative Art Tools and Techniques**

- Processing is an open-source programming language and integrated development environment (IDE) designed specifically for the visual arts. It provides a flexible platform for artists to create generative art through code, enabling the creation of complex and dynamic visual expressions. Its simplicity and accessibility make it a popular choice for beginners and experienced coders.

- Midjourney is an AI-driven platform that generates high-quality images from text prompts. It leverages advanced machine learning models to interpret and visualise user inputs, making it a powerful tool for concept artists and designers.

- Stable Diffusion is an AI model that generates images based on textual descriptions. It is handy for creating detailed and coherent images from complex prompts, making it a valuable tool for illustrators and visual storytellers.

## Examples of Generative Artists

**Refik Anadol:** Refik Anadol is a media artist known for using AI and machine learning to create immersive art installations. His work, "Melting Memories," uses brainwave data to create stunning visual representations of memory, blurring the lines between art, science, and technology.

**Mario Klingemann:** Mario Klingemann is a pioneer in AI art, using neural networks to create generative artworks. His piece, "Memories of Passersby I," features two AI models generating an endless stream of portraits in real-time, challenging traditional notions of authorship and creativity.

**Sofia Crespo:** Sofia Crespo's work explores the intersection of biology and technology, using AI to create intricate and surreal representations of nature. Her series "Neural Zoo" features AI-generated images of imaginary creatures, blending the natural world with artificial intelligence.

## Ethical Considerations in AI-Driven Design

As AI becomes more integrated into the design process, it brings ethical considerations that designers must address. Here are some key ethical issues to consider:

**Bias and Fairness:** AI models can inherit biases from the data they are trained on, leading to unfair and discriminatory outcomes. To minimise bias, designers must ensure their AI systems are trained on diverse and representative data sets. Regular audits and evaluations can help identify and mitigate biases in AI-driven designs.

**Transparency and Accountability:** Designers must be transparent about how AI systems are used in the design process and ensure accountability for their outcomes. This includes explaining how AI-generated decisions are made and providing mechanisms for users to challenge or appeal those decisions.

**Privacy and Data Security:** AI systems often rely on large amounts of user data, raising concerns about privacy and data security. Designers must implement robust data protection measures and ensure compliance with privacy regulations. Transparency about data collection and usage practices is crucial to maintaining user trust.

**Intellectual Property:** The use of AI-generated content raises intellectual property rights issues. Designers must navigate the legal landscape to determine ownership and usage rights for AI-generated designs. Clear agreements and policies can address these issues and protect the interests of all parties involved.

**Human-AI Collaboration:** Integrating AI into the design process should enhance human creativity rather than replace it. Designers must balance leveraging AI capabilities and maintaining human oversight and control. Emphasising AI's collaborative nature ensures that it complements and enhances human creativity.

## Leveraging AI to Design and Scale Products

AI offers immense potential for designing and scaling products. Here are some strategies for leveraging AI in product design and development:

**Rapid Prototyping:** AI can quickly accelerate prototyping by generating multiple design iterations. Tools like Autodesk's Fusion 360 use AI to create design variations based on specified parameters, allowing designers to explore different options and refine their ideas faster.

**User-Centred Design:** AI can analyse user data to gain insights into user needs, preferences, and behaviours. This information can inform the design process, ensuring that products are tailored to meet user expectations. For example, AI-driven user research tools can analyse feedback and sentiment to identify pain points and opportunities for improvement.

**Predictive Analytics:** AI can predict future trends and user behaviours, helping designers anticipate market demands and create products that resonate with users. Predictive analytics can also optimise inventory management, pricing strategies, and marketing campaigns, ensuring that products are well-received and profitable.

**Scalability and Efficiency:** Integrating AI with design systems to automate routine tasks, generate components, and maintain consistency across digital products. AI tools can quickly process and apply design system rules, significantly reducing the time spent on tasks like code generation and style consistency checks. This allows designers to focus more on creative and strategic aspects of their work.

**Customisation and Personalization:** AI enables mass customisation and personalisation, allowing companies to offer tailored products to individual users. AI-driven design tools can create unique product configurations based on user preferences, enhancing the customer experience and increasing brand loyalty.

## AI in Design Leadership

AI is also reshaping design leadership by providing new tools and insights to enhance decision-making and strategy. Here's how AI is impacting design leadership:

**Informed Decision-Making:** AI provides leaders with data-driven insights to inform strategic decisions. By analysing trends, user behaviour, and performance metrics, AI helps leaders make informed choices about design direction, resource allocation, and project prioritisation.

**Enhanced Collaboration:** AI tools can facilitate collaboration by providing real-time feedback, automating routine tasks, and generating data-driven insights. This allows teams to work more efficiently and focus on high-value creative work. Collaborative platforms like Figma and Miro integrate AI features to enhance team workflows and productivity.

**Talent Management:** AI can assist in talent management by analysing performance data, identifying skill gaps, and recommending professional development opportunities. This helps leaders build high-performing teams and ensure their designers continuously grow and develop their skills.

**Innovation and Experimentation:** AI encourages innovation and experimentation by providing new tools and capabilities. Design leaders can leverage AI to explore new creative directions, test hypotheses, and iterate on designs quickly. This fosters a culture of continuous improvement and innovation within the design team.

**Resource Optimization:** AI can optimise resource management by analysing project data, predicting workload, and recommending resource allocation. This helps leaders manage their teams more effectively and ensure that projects are completed on time and within budget.

**Addressing Concerns About AI and Job Displacement**

A common concern about AI is that it will replace human jobs, including those in creative fields like design. However, the reality is more nuanced. AI is not here to steal jobs but to enhance and augment human capabilities. Here's how AI can be a powerful enabler for designers:

**Empowering Designers:** AI empowers designers by automating repetitive tasks and providing new tools for creativity. This allows designers to focus on higher-level strategic and creative work, enhancing their productivity and job satisfaction.

**Creating New Opportunities:** AI creates new opportunities for designers by opening up new fields and applications. For example, generative art, AI-driven user research, and personalised design experiences are emerging areas where designers can apply their skills and expertise.

**Enhancing Creativity:** AI enhances creativity by providing fresh perspectives, generating new ideas, and offering insights based on vast amounts of data. Designers can leverage AI to explore new creative directions and push the boundaries of traditional design.

**Continuous Learning:** AI tools often include features that help designers learn and improve their skills. For example, AI-driven feedback systems can provide real-time critiques and suggestions, assisting designers in refining their work and developing their expertise.

**Collaborative Partnership:** AI should be viewed as a collaborative partner rather than a competitor. By working alongside AI, designers can achieve more than they could on their own, leveraging the strengths of both human creativity and machine intelligence.

## Case Studies: AI in Design and Product Development

To illustrate the impact of AI in design and product development, let's explore some case studies from leading companies and designers:

### Case Study 1: IBM Watson and Design

IBM Watson is a powerful AI platform used in various design applications. One notable example is Watson's collaboration with the fashion industry. Watson analysed thousands of fashion images and trends to create a unique collection for the 2016 Met Gala. The AI-generated designs were well-received, demonstrating how AI can assist in creative processes and generate innovative ideas.

### Case Study 2: Adobe Sensei

Adobe Sensei is an AI and machine learning framework integrated into Adobe's suite of design tools. Sensei automates repetitive tasks, provides design recommendations, and enhances creative workflows. For example, Sensei's content-aware fill feature in Photoshop allows designers to remove unwanted image elements seamlessly. Sensei's capabilities demonstrate how AI can augment creativity and improve design efficiency.

## Case Study 3: Spotify's Personalised Playlists

Spotify leverages AI to create personalised music experiences for users. The "Discover Weekly" feature uses machine learning algorithms to analyse user listening habits and recommend new music. This AI-driven personalisation has been a significant factor in Spotify's success, enhancing user engagement and satisfaction. Spotify's approach showcases how AI can create tailored experiences that resonate with users.

## Frameworks for Integrating AI into Design

To effectively integrate AI into your design process, consider adopting the following frameworks:

### The AI-Driven Design Process

- **Ideation:** Use AI tools to generate ideas and explore new creative directions. AI can analyse existing designs, trends, and user data to provide fresh perspectives and inspire innovative concepts.

- **Prototyping:** Leverage AI to accelerate the prototyping process. AI-driven tools can create multiple design iterations based on specified parameters, allowing designers to experiment and refine their ideas quickly.

- **User Research:** Use AI to gather and analyse user data. AI-driven user research tools can provide insights into user needs, preferences, and behaviours, informing the design process and ensuring that products are user-centred.

- **Design Optimization:** Apply AI to optimise design decisions. AI can provide recommendations and insights based on data analysis, helping designers make informed choices and improve the overall design.

- **Testing and Validation:** Use AI to test and validate designs. AI-driven testing tools can simulate user interactions and provide feedback on usability and performance, ensuring that designs meet user expectations.

## The Human-AI Collaboration Framework

- **Define Roles and Responsibilities:** Clearly define human designers' and AI systems' roles and responsibilities. Establish guidelines for how AI will be used in the design process and ensure that human oversight and control are maintained.

- **Emphasise Collaboration:** Foster a collaborative environment where AI is seen as a tool to augment human creativity. Encourage designers to leverage AI capabilities to explore new possibilities and enhance their work.

- **Continuous Learning:** Invest in continuous learning and development for designers. Provide training and resources to help designers develop their AI skills and stay informed about the latest advancements.

- **Ethical Considerations:** Address ethical considerations related to AI use in design. Ensure transparency, fairness, and accountability in AI-driven design decisions: Prioritise user privacy and data security.

- **Iterative Improvement:** Continuously iterate and improve AI systems based on user feedback and performance data. Regularly evaluate AI's impact on the design process and adjust as needed.

## Practical Applications: Embracing AI in Design

To fully embrace AI in your design practice, consider the following practical applications:

### Invest in AI Tools and Technologies

Invest in AI tools and technologies that enhance your design capabilities. This could include AI-driven design software, machine learning platforms, and data analysis tools. Ensure that your team has access to the tools they need to leverage AI effectively.

Examples of popular AI tools for designers include Adobe Sensei, Autodesk Dreamcatcher, and Runway ML. These tools provide valuable capabilities to enhance creativity, improve efficiency, and optimise design decisions.

## Collaborate with AI Experts

Collaborate with AI experts, data scientists, and engineers to enhance your AI-driven design efforts. These professionals can provide valuable insights, help interpret complex data, and guide you in implementing AI solutions.

One designer mentioned, "Working with AI experts has transformed our design process. Their machine learning and data analysis expertise has helped us uncover deeper insights and create more innovative designs."

## Stay Informed About AI Advancements

Stay informed about the latest advancements in AI and machine learning. Follow industry blogs, attend conferences, and participate in webinars to stay current with new tools, techniques, and case studies. Staying informed will help you continuously improve your AI skills and remain competitive.

## Experiment and Innovate

Experiment with AI-driven tools and techniques to explore new creative possibilities. Use AI to push the boundaries of traditional design and create innovative solutions that were previously unimaginable.

One of my mentees shared, "AI has opened up new creative avenues I never thought possible. By experimenting with AI-driven tools, I've been able to create designs that are truly unique and impactful."

## Conclusion: AI and the Creative Process

AI is revolutionising the design industry, offering new tools and capabilities that enhance creativity and efficiency. By integrating AI into the design process, designers can generate innovative ideas, optimise design decisions, and create personalised user experiences. However, addressing ethical considerations and maintaining human oversight and control in AI-driven design is essential.

Embrace AI's potential to transform your design practice. Invest in AI tools and technologies, collaborate with experts, and stay informed about the latest advancements. By leveraging AI, you can enhance your creativity, improve design efficiency, and create products that resonate with users.

AI is not here to replace designers but to empower them. It opens up new possibilities, enhances human creativity, and enables designers to achieve more. By viewing AI as a collaborator rather than a competitor, we can harness its potential to create designs that truly stand out and make a lasting impact.

# CHAPTER 15

## Immersive Realities: AR, VR, and Intelligent Interfaces

The design world is expanding beyond traditional screens into immersive realities powered by Augmented Reality (AR), Virtual Reality (VR), and intelligent interfaces. These technologies are revolutionising how we interact with digital and physical spaces, offering new opportunities for creativity, innovation, and engagement. This chapter delves into the significance of AR, VR, and intelligent interfaces, explores frameworks for designing these experiences, and examines their potential to shape the future of design.

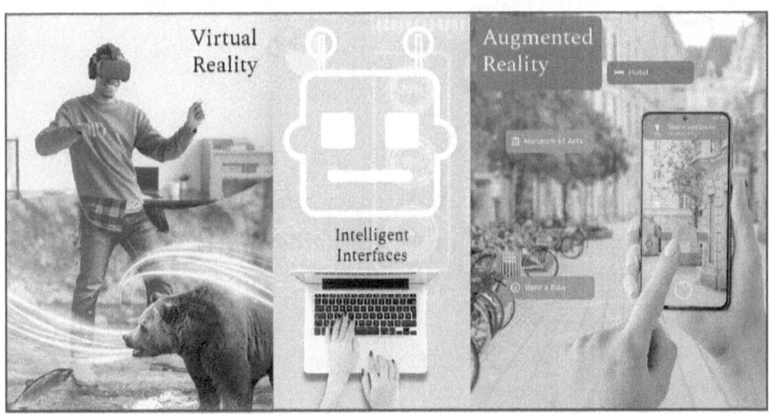

**The Importance of AR, VR, and Intelligent Interfaces**

**Enhanced User Experiences:** These technologies create more engaging and interactive user experiences. AR overlays digital content onto the real world, while VR immerses users in entirely virtual environments. Intelligent interfaces adapt to user needs, providing personalised and intuitive interactions.

**New Creative Possibilities:** AR, VR, and intelligent interfaces open new creative avenues. Designers can create previously unimaginable experiences, blending the digital and physical worlds in innovative ways.

**Improved Learning and Training:** These technologies are being used to enhance education and training by providing immersive, hands-on experiences. For example, VR can simulate complex scenarios for medical training, while AR can offer interactive learning aids in classrooms.

**Increased Accessibility:** Intelligent interfaces can make technology more accessible to people with disabilities. For instance, voice-activated assistants can help users with mobility impairments, while AR can provide real-time translations for individuals with hearing impairments.

**Future-Proofing:** As AR, VR, and intelligent interfaces continue to evolve, they will play an increasingly important role in our daily lives. Designers who embrace these technologies now will be better positioned to create innovative solutions and stay ahead of industry trends.

## The Applications of AR, VR, and Intelligent Interfaces

Augmented Reality (AR), Virtual Reality (VR), and intelligent interfaces are on a trajectory that promises to reshape our world profoundly. With continuous advancements, these technologies are set to revolutionise how we interact with the digital and physical worlds. Here's a deeper dive into the key trends and developments shaping this exciting frontier:

### Mixed Reality (MR): Bridging the Digital and Physical Worlds

Mixed Reality (MR) is an emerging technology that seamlessly blends elements of AR and VR. Unlike AR, which overlays digital information in the real world, or VR, which immerses users in a completely virtual environment, MR allows physical and digital objects to coexist and interact in real-time. This convergence has the potential to revolutionise several industries:

- **Healthcare:** Imagine surgeons performing complex procedures with real-time digital overlays guiding them or patients receiving remote diagnoses through virtual consultations that feel almost as personal as in-person visits. Microsoft's HoloLens 2 is already used in operating rooms to provide surgeons 3D visualisations of patient anatomy.

- **Education:** MR can transform learning by bringing abstract concepts to life. Students could explore historical sites virtually or conduct science experiments in a controlled yet interactive environment. For example, the "Merge EDU" app allows students to hold and interact with digital objects, enhancing their understanding of complex concepts.

- **Entertainment:** The entertainment industry stands to benefit immensely from MR, offering audiences immersive and interactive experiences, from live concerts to gaming.

## Artificial Intelligence (AI) Integration: Making Interfaces Smarter

Integrating AI with AR, VR, and intelligent interfaces enhances responsiveness and adaptability. AI-driven technologies can personalise user experiences and provide more intuitive interactions:

- **Intelligent Avatars:** In VR environments, AI can create avatars that mimic human behaviours and adapt to user preferences, making virtual interactions more realistic and engaging. Meta's Horizon Workrooms use AI to create realistic avatars that can mimic facial expressions and gestures during virtual meetings.

- **Personalised Recommendations:** In AR applications, AI can analyse user data to offer tailored suggestions, guide shoppers to their preferred products, or provide contextual information based on real-time interactions. Snapchat's AR filters use AI to give users custom effects and recommendations based on their preferences and behaviour.

## Wearable Technology: Enhancing Accessibility and Comfort

Wearable technology, such as AR glasses and VR headsets, is evolving rapidly. These devices are becoming lighter, more powerful, and affordable, making immersive experiences more accessible to a broader audience:

- **Next-Generation AR Glasses:** Sleek, lightweight AR glasses that blend seamlessly into everyday life are on the horizon. They promise to keep users connected and informed without the bulk and obtrusiveness of current models. Google's Project Iris aims to create AR glasses that are both stylish and functional, offering a blend of digital and real-world information.

- **Advanced VR Headsets:** VR headsets are becoming more ergonomic and feature-rich. They offer higher resolutions, more expansive fields of view, and improved motion tracking, enhancing user comfort and immersion. The Oculus Quest 2 is a prime example, providing a high-quality VR experience with untethered mobility and an affordable price point.

## Haptic Feedback: Adding the Sense of Touch

Haptic feedback technology is advancing, providing users with tactile sensations that make digital interactions feel more lifelike:

- **Training Simulations:** In fields like medicine and aviation, haptic feedback can create realistic training environments where professionals can hone their skills without real-world risks. For instance, the HaptX Gloves offer realistic touch feedback, allowing users to feel virtual objects with high precision.

- **Gaming:** For gamers, haptic feedback can add a new dimension of realism, allowing them to feel the impact of actions within the game, thus deepening their engagement. Sony's PlayStation 5 DualSense controller provides dynamic haptic feedback that varies with in-game actions, enhancing the gaming experience.

- **Virtual Prototyping:** Designers and engineers can manipulate virtual models using haptic feedback to understand better how products feel and function before production. Companies like Tesla use haptic feedback in VR to test and refine their designs before manufacturing.

## Frameworks for Designing Immersive Experiences

Designing for AR, VR, and intelligent interfaces requires a different approach than traditional design. Here are some frameworks to guide you:

User-Centred Design (UCD): UCD is a design philosophy that places the user at the centre of the design process. This means understanding the user's context, needs, and limitations for AR, VR, and intelligent interfaces to create intuitive and engaging experiences.

**Immersive Experience Design:** This framework creates seamless, engaging, and user-friendly immersive experiences. Key elements include spatial design, interaction design, and narrative design. Spatial design considers how users move and interact within a space, while interaction design focuses on how users interact with the digital elements. Narrative design involves creating compelling stories that guide users through the experience.

**Prototyping and Iteration:** Rapid prototyping and iteration are crucial for designing immersive experiences. Use tools like Unity, Unreal Engine, and ARKit to create and test prototypes with users. Gather feedback and make necessary adjustments to improve the user experience.

**Accessibility and Inclusivity:** Ensure your designs are accessible to all users, regardless of their abilities. This includes considering visual, auditory, and mobility impairments. Use frameworks like the Web Content Accessibility Guidelines (WCAG) and the Inclusive Design Principles to guide your efforts.

**Ethical Design:** Consider the ethical implications of your designs. This includes user privacy, data security, and the potential for addiction or overuse. Be transparent about how data is collected and used, and design experiences that promote healthy usage patterns.

## Designing for Intelligent Systems

Intelligent interfaces are powered by AI and machine learning, enabling them to adapt to user needs and provide personalised experiences. Here are key considerations and frameworks for designing intelligent systems:

**Context Awareness:** Intelligent interfaces should know the user's context, including their location, preferences, and previous interactions. This allows the system to provide relevant and timely information and suggestions.

**Personalisation:** Use AI to personalise the user experience based on data collected about the user's behaviour and preferences. This can include personalised content recommendations, customised interfaces, and adaptive learning paths.

**Natural Interaction:** Design intelligent interfaces to support natural modes of interaction, such as voice, gesture, and touch. This makes the system more intuitive and easier to use.

**Transparency and Control:** The system should be transparent about how it uses data and give users control over their personal information. Users should be able to customise their settings and preferences to ensure they feel comfortable and in control.

**Ethical AI:** To avoid bias, ensure your AI models are trained on diverse and representative datasets. Regularly audit your systems for fairness and transparency, and consider the ethical implications of your designs.

## Case Studies of Intelligent Interfaces

**Voice Assistants (Google Assistant, Siri, Alexa):** These voice-activated assistants use AI to understand and respond to user queries, providing a hands-free and intuitive interface. They can perform a wide range of tasks, from setting reminders to controlling smart home devices.

**Netflix Personalisation Engine:** Netflix uses AI to provide personalised content recommendations based on users' viewing habits. This enhances the user experience by making it easier for users to find enjoyable content.

**Tesla's Autopilot system:** This system uses AI to assist with driving, providing features such as lane-keeping, adaptive cruise control, and self-parking. The system continuously learns and improves based on data collected from Tesla vehicles worldwide.

**Apple Surgical Settings:** The Apple Vision Pro shows excellent potential in surgical environments, providing surgeons with real-time imaging and augmented reality (AR) guidance. This platform enhances precision, minimises procedural errors, and improves patient outcomes by overlaying preoperative imaging data directly in the surgical field.

## Ethical Considerations and Challenges

As with any emerging technology, AR, VR, and intelligent interfaces come with ethical considerations and challenges that designers must address:

**Privacy and Security:** These technologies often collect and process large amounts of personal data. Implementing robust security measures and being transparent about data usage is crucial. Ensure users have control of their data and understand how it is used.

**Digital Addiction:** The immersive nature of AR and VR can lead to excessive use and addiction. Design experiences that promote healthy usage patterns and include features encouraging users to take breaks and manage their time.

**Bias and Inclusivity:** Intelligent interfaces can inherit biases from the data they are trained on, leading to discriminatory outcomes. Ensure that your AI models are trained on diverse and representative datasets, and regularly audit your systems for bias. This applies to AR and VR experiences where the hardware of modalities also tends to create bias.

**Physical and Mental Health:** Prolonged use of VR headsets can cause physical discomfort, such as eye strain and motion sickness. Be mindful of these issues and design experiences that minimise their impact. Additionally, consider the potential mental health effects of immersive experiences and provide resources for users who may be affected.

**Ethical Design:** Consider the broader ethical implications of your designs. For example, how might your AR application impact the physical environment or the behaviour of its users? Strive to create experiences that are engaging but also responsible and respectful of societal norms and values.

## Conclusion: Embracing Immersive Realities

AR, VR, and intelligent interfaces represent the next frontier in design, offering unprecedented opportunities for creativity, innovation, and engagement. By embracing these technologies and incorporating them into your design practice, you can create experiences that are not only immersive and interactive but also inclusive and ethical.

As designers, it is our responsibility to thoughtfully and responsibly shape the future of these technologies. By following best practices, leveraging frameworks, and continuously learning and iterating, we can harness the power of AR, VR, and intelligent interfaces to create meaningful and impactful experiences.

Embrace the possibilities, push the boundaries, and let your creativity soar in this exciting new landscape.

# CHAPTER 16

# The Business of Design: Balancing Creativity and Commerce

Design is not just an art; it is a powerful business tool. Design can transform businesses, create value, and drive innovation when leveraged correctly. This chapter explores the intersection of design and business, offering insights into how designers can effectively communicate value, align design with business goals, and navigate the commercial aspects of the design industry.

## The Intersection of Design and Business

Designers are often at the crossroads of creativity and commerce. While the artistic aspect of design drives innovation and user engagement, the business aspect ensures that these innovations are viable and profitable. Designers must understand and align with business objectives to navigate this intersection successfully.

### Understanding Business Goals

Designers must immerse themselves in the business context to contribute meaningfully. This involves understanding the company's mission, vision, and key performance indicators (KPIs). Engaging with business leaders and stakeholders is crucial to comprehend how design can support and amplify business objectives.

For instance, consider a company looking to improve customer retention. A designer will have to translate this goal into creating a more intuitive user interface for their app, ensuring a seamless user experience that keeps customers engaged and reduces churn. By aligning their work with such strategic objectives, designers can ensure their contributions are creative and impactful.

## Communicating Design Value

One of the most significant challenges designers face is articulating the value of design to non-design stakeholders. This requires translating design benefits into business metrics. Instead of focusing solely on the aesthetic aspects, highlight how design improvements can enhance user experience, boost customer satisfaction, and drive sales.

Use concrete examples and metrics to effectively communicate the value of design. For instance, if a website redesign led to a 20% increase in user engagement and a 15% boost in sales, these metrics can powerfully convey the tangible benefits of design. Additionally, case studies from successful companies can illustrate the transformative impact of design on business outcomes.

## Case Study: Airbnb

Airbnb has effectively integrated design into its business strategy. The founders' design backgrounds ensured design thinking was embedded in the company's DNA. This focus on user-centred design has led to innovative solutions and a seamless user experience, contributing significantly to Airbnb's success and market differentiation.

By prioritising design, Airbnb created a platform that is not only functional but also delightful to use. The emphasis on intuitive design and user feedback has enabled Airbnb to continuously improve its service, attract a broad user base, and maintain a competitive edge in the hospitality industry.

## Aligning Design with Business Strategy

Aligning design with business strategy ensures that creative efforts are innovative and strategically impactful. This alignment involves integrating design thinking into the business strategy and ensuring the design is part of all significant business decisions.

## Collaborative Approach

Effective collaboration between designers and business teams is essential. This involves regular communication, shared goals, and mutual respect for each other's expertise. Tools like design briefs, regular check-ins, and collaborative workshops can facilitate this process.

## The Design Brief

A design brief is a document that outlines the objectives, scope, and deliverables of a design project. It serves as a roadmap for designers and business stakeholders, ensuring everyone is aligned on the project goals.

Key Components of a Design Brief Include:

**Project Overview:** This is a summary of the project, including its purpose and objectives. It sets the stage for the project and provides context for all stakeholders.

**Target Audience:** Detailed information about the end-users of the product or service. Understanding the audience is crucial for creating user-centred designs.

**Scope of Work:** This section provides a clear outline of the tasks and deliverables. It defines the project's boundaries, ensuring everyone understands what is included and what is not.

**Timeline:** Key milestones and deadlines. A well-defined timeline helps keep the project on track and ensures all tasks are completed on time.

**Budget:** Financial constraints and resources allocated for the project. Understanding the budget helps make informed decisions about design choices and resource allocation.

**Success Metrics:** Criteria for measuring the project's success. Determining success metrics ensures that the team has a clear understanding of what constitutes a successful outcome.

A well-crafted design brief fosters clear communication and alignment, ensuring that design and business objectives are met.

## The Economics of Design

Understanding the economics of design involves recognising the financial impact of design decisions and how design contributes to overall profitability. This includes cost considerations, pricing strategies, and return on investment (ROI).

### Cost Considerations

Design projects can be expensive, involving research, prototyping, testing, and implementation costs. Designers must be mindful of these costs and work within budgets. This may involve making trade-offs or finding cost-effective solutions that maintain quality.

### Framework: Cost-Benefit Analysis

Cost-benefit analysis (CBA) evaluates the costs and benefits of a design project. It helps determine whether the benefits outweigh the costs and aids in making informed decisions.

### Steps to Conduct a CBA:

- **Identify Costs:** List all the costs associated with the project, including direct costs (e.g., materials, labour) and indirect costs (e.g., overhead). This comprehensive cost assessment ensures that all expenses are accounted for.

- **Identify Benefits:** List all the benefits, both tangible (e.g., increased sales) and intangible (e.g., improved customer satisfaction). Identifying benefits helps understand the total value the design project can bring.

- **Quantify Costs and Benefits:** Assign monetary values to the costs and benefits. Quantifying these values allows a direct comparison of costs and benefits.

- **Calculate Net Benefit:** Subtract the total costs from the total benefits to determine the net benefit. The net benefit clearly indicates whether the project is financially viable.

Designers can make informed decisions that balance creative aspirations with financial realities by conducting a CBA.

## Pricing Strategies: Valuing Your Creative Work

Pricing design services is one of the most challenging yet crucial aspects of running a successful design business. The right pricing strategy can significantly impact profitability, client satisfaction, and market positioning. Setting the right pricing strategy is very important for design agencies and freelancers. This can include hourly rates, project-based pricing, or value-based pricing. Designers can choose from several pricing models, each with advantages and challenges. Selecting a model that aligns with your business goals, project types, and client expectations is vital.

## Hourly Rate

Charging by the hour is a straightforward approach. Clients pay for the time spent on a project. This model is suitable for projects with uncertain scopes or ongoing work.

**Advantages:**

- **Transparency:** Clients can see exactly what they are paying.

- **Flexibility:** Ideal for projects with evolving requirements.

**Challenges:**

- **Time Tracking:** Requires meticulous tracking of hours worked.

- **Potential for Disputes:** Clients might question the time spent on tasks.

**Framework for Setting an Hourly Rate:**

- **Calculate Your Costs:** Include all business expenses (software, hardware, office space, etc.).

- **Determine Your Desired Salary:** Decide how much you need to earn annually.

- **Estimate Billable Hours:** Calculate the hours you can realistically bill clients annually.

- **Set Your Rate:** Use the formula:

$$\text{Hourly Rate} = \frac{\text{Annual Salary} + \text{Business Expenses}}{\text{Billable Hours}}$$

For example, if your annual salary goal is $60,000 and your business expenses are $20,000, with 1,500 billable hours per year, your hourly rate would be:

$$\text{Hourly Rate} = \frac{\$60,000 + \$20,000}{\$1,500} = \$53.33$$

### Project-Based Pricing

Project-based pricing involves setting a fixed price for the entire project. This model works well for well-defined projects with clear deliverables.

**Advantages:**

- **Clarity for Clients:** Clients know the total cost upfront.

- **Potential for Higher Profit:** Efficient work can lead to higher effective hourly rates.

**Challenges:**

- **Scope Creep:** Unclear project scopes can lead to additional work without extra pay.

- **Risk of Underpricing:** Misestimating the time required can cause lower profitability.

Framework for Project-Based Pricing:

- **Define the Project Scope:** Clearly outline the tasks, deliverables, and timeline.

- **Estimate Hours:** Calculate the total hours required to complete the project.

- **Apply Hourly Rate:** Multiply the estimated hours by your hourly rate.

- **Add a Buffer:** Include a contingency amount to cover unexpected issues (typically 10-20%).

For example, if a website redesign project is estimated to take 100 hours, and your hourly rate is $50, you might price the project at:

$$\text{Project Price} = 100 \times 50 + (0.1 \times 100 \times 50) = \$5,500$$

## Value-Based Pricing

Value-based pricing sets prices based on the perceived value to the client rather than the cost of production. This model is beneficial when your work significantly impacts the client's business.

Advantages:

- **Potential for Higher Fees:** Prices reflect the value delivered, not just the time spent.

- **Client Focus:** Emphasises results and benefits for the client.

Challenges:

- **Requires Strong Justification:** Clients must understand and agree with the value provided.

- **Difficult to Standardise:** Each project might require a different valuation approach.

**Framework for Value-Based Pricing:**

- **Understand Client Goals:** Learn about the client's business objectives and how your work will impact them.

- **Quantify the Value:** Estimate the financial benefits your design will bring to the client (e.g., increased sales, improved brand perception).

- **Set the Price:** Determine a fee that reflects a fair portion of the value delivered.

For example, if a new branding strategy is projected to increase a client's revenue by $100,000, you might set a price at 10% of the projected revenue increase.

## Negotiating Prices

Effective negotiation ensures you and your client are satisfied with the agreement. Here are some tips for successful price negotiations:

**Know Your Worth:** Understand the value of your work and be confident in your pricing. Clients are more likely to accept your rates if they sense you are confident and knowledgeable about the value you bring.

**Be Transparent:** Clearly explain how you arrived at your price. Break down the costs and justify your rates with data and examples. Transparency builds trust and helps clients understand the value of your services.

**Offer Flexible Options:** Provide clients with different pricing options, such as a tiered pricing structure with varying service levels. This flexibility can make your services more accessible and attractive to a broader range of clients.

**Prepare for Objections:** Anticipate potential objections and prepare responses. For example, if a client thinks your rate is too high, explain the benefits and return on investment they can expect from your work.

**Be Willing to Walk Away:** Sometimes, a client may need to be more willing to pay what your services are worth. In such cases, be prepared to leave. Undervaluing your work can lead to resentment and financial strain.

## Practical Advice for Setting and Adjusting Prices

### Regularly Review Your Rates

Periodically review and adjust your rates to reflect your skill level, experience, and market demand changes. Staying competitive requires being up-to-date with industry standards and adjusting your pricing accordingly.

### Consider Market Conditions

Understand market conditions and their impact on pricing. In high-demand periods, you might increase your rates. Conversely, you might offer discounts or package deals during slower periods to attract clients.

### Build a Pricing Portfolio

Create a portfolio that includes different pricing packages tailored to various client needs. This can help you cater to a broader range of clients and offer them services that fit their budget while ensuring profitability.

### Gather Feedback

Seek customer feedback on your pricing. Understanding their perspective can provide valuable insights and help you refine your pricing strategy.

### Educate Clients

Educate clients about the value of design and the benefits they can expect. An informed client will appreciate your work and agree to your pricing.

## Positioning Design as a Business Asset

For design to be recognised as a critical component of business success, it must be positioned as a strategic asset. This involves demonstrating how design contributes to business goals and advocating for design at the highest levels of the organisation.

### Building a Design-Driven Culture

A design-driven culture values design at every level of the organisation. This involves fostering a mindset that appreciates the role of design in driving innovation and solving business problems. Leaders should advocate for design, invest in design talent, and ensure that design is integrated into decision-making.

**Case Study: Tesla**

Tesla's success is partly attributed to its strong focus on design. Design is integral to Tesla's brand, from the sleek aesthetics of its vehicles to the seamless user experience of its digital interfaces and the introduction of an online car-buying experience. This focus on design has helped Tesla stand out in the automotive industry and build a loyal customer base.

By prioritising design, Tesla has created products that are not only technologically advanced but also visually appealing and user-friendly. This emphasis on design has contributed significantly to Tesla's market differentiation and success.

**Framework: Building a Design-Driven Culture**

Steps to build a design-driven culture:

**Leadership Buy-In:** Ensure that top executives understand and support the value of design. Leadership support is crucial for fostering a culture that values design.

**Design Advocacy:** Advocate for design at all levels of the organisation, demonstrating its impact on business outcomes. Design advocacy ensures that design is integrated into strategic discussions and decision-making processes.

**Invest in Talent:** Hire and retain top design talent, providing them with the resources and support they need to succeed. Investing in talent ensures that the organisation has the skills and expertise required to drive innovation.

**Integrated Processes:** Integrate design into the organisation's core processes, from product development to marketing. This ensures that design is considered in all major business decisions.

**Continuous Learning:** Foster a continuous learning and improvement culture, encouraging designers to stay current with industry trends and best practices. Continuous learning ensures that the organisation remains at the forefront of design innovation.

Building a design-driven culture requires commitment and effort, but it can lead to significant benefits in terms of innovation, customer satisfaction, and business success.

## Navigating Commercial Aspects of Design

Designers often face challenges when navigating the commercial aspects of their work. This includes understanding contracts, managing client relationships, and ensuring intellectual property rights.

### Understanding Contracts

Contracts are essential for protecting both designers and clients. They should clearly outline the scope of work, timelines, deliverables, payment terms, and intellectual property rights. Designers should be familiar with contract terms and ensure they have legally binding agreements before starting work.

A well-drafted contract helps set clear expectations and avoid misunderstandings. It also provides legal protection and ensures that both parties are aware of their responsibilities and obligations.

## Key Elements of a Design Contract

**Scope of Work:** Clearly define the project's scope, including specific tasks, deliverables, and any exclusions. A detailed scope of work helps prevent scope creep, where additional tasks are added without additional compensation.

**Timelines and Milestones:** Outline the project timeline, including key milestones and deadlines. This ensures that both parties clearly understand the project schedule and can plan accordingly.

**Payment Terms:** Specify the payment structure, including the total cost, payment schedule, and any penalties for late payment. This can include upfront deposits, milestone payments, and final payment upon project completion.

**Intellectual Property Rights:** Clarify the ownership of the work created. This includes whether the designer retains ownership of the designs or transfers the rights to the client upon payment.

**Revisions and Changes:** Define the process for handling revisions and changes to the project. This includes the number of revisions included in the initial cost and the cost for additional revisions.

**Termination Clause:** Include a clause outlining the conditions under which either party can terminate the contract. This provides a clear exit strategy in case the project needs to be halted.

**Confidentiality Agreement:** If necessary, include a confidentiality agreement to protect sensitive information shared during the project.

## Managing Client Relationships

Effective client management is crucial for successful design projects. This involves clear communication, setting realistic expectations, and maintaining professionalism. Regular updates and feedback loops help ensure the project stays on track and meets client expectations.

Building trust with clients is essential for a successful working relationship. This involves being transparent, delivering on promises, and demonstrating a genuine interest in the client's business goals.

**Example:** Consider a design agency working with a new client on a website redesign. The agency holds regular meetings with the client to discuss progress, gather feedback, and address concerns. The agency builds a strong relationship based on trust and mutual respect by maintaining open lines of communication and being responsive to the client's needs. This leads to a successful project and opens the door for future collaborations.

## The Importance of Building Strong Client Relationships

Beyond the legalities and formalities of contracts lies the heart of successful design projects: strong client relationships. Developing and maintaining a positive rapport with clients is crucial for the smooth execution of projects, repeat business and referrals. Here's how you can build and nurture these relationships.

**Building Trust and Credibility:** Trust is the foundation of any successful client relationship. Clients must feel confident in your abilities and know you have their best interests at heart. This trust is built over time through consistent communication, reliability, and delivering quality work.

**Communication is Key:** Open, honest, and frequent communication is vital. From the initial consultation to project completion, keeping clients informed about progress, challenges, and milestones helps build a transparent relationship. Regular updates prevent misunderstandings and ensure both sides are aligned.

**Reliability and Consistency:** Meeting deadlines, sticking to agreed budgets, and consistently delivering high-quality work build your reputation as a reliable designer. When clients know they can depend on you, they are more likely to return for future projects and recommend your services to others.

**Setting Realistic Expectations:** At the start of any project, it's important to set realistic expectations regarding timelines, costs, and deliverables. This honesty helps avoid disappointments and misunderstandings later on.

**Clear Project Scope:** Clearly define the project's scope, including specific deliverables, timelines, and costs. Discuss and document any additional requests or changes to ensure mutual understanding and agreement.

**Managing Changes and Revisions:** Clients may request changes or revisions as the project progresses. It's important to handle these requests professionally. Define how many revisions are included in the original scope and how additional changes will be billed. This clarity helps manage expectations and prevents scope creep.

**Example:** A freelance designer working on a website redesign sets clear expectations with the client. They outline the project scope, including the number of revisions allowed. The designer explains the extra costs when the client requests changes beyond the agreed scope. This professional approach helps maintain a positive relationship while ensuring the project stays on track.

## Enriching Client Relationships with Empathy

Empathy is crucial in understanding and addressing client needs. By putting yourself in the client's shoes, you can better appreciate their challenges, goals, and perspectives.

**Understanding Client Needs and Goals:** Take the time to understand the client's business, market, and target audience. This deeper understanding allows you to create designs that meet and exceed client expectations.

**Going the Extra Mile:** Exceeding client expectations can sometimes leave a lasting impression and lead to long-term business relationships.

**Delivering More than Expected:** Going the extra mile can significantly boost client satisfaction, whether it's providing additional design concepts, faster turnaround times, or unexpected enhancements.

**Emotional Intelligence:** Use emotional intelligence to navigate client interactions. Recognise and respond to clients' emotional cues, whether they are stressed about a deadline or excited about a new idea. This empathetic approach can strengthen your professional relationships.

**Example:** A UX designer working with a non-profit organisation takes extra time to understand the emotional impact of the organisation's mission. By attending a few of their events and speaking with volunteers and beneficiaries, the designer gains valuable insights that inform a more empathetic and practical design, ultimately leading to a more robust user experience.

## Handling Feedback and Constructive Criticism

Feedback is a vital part of the design process. Handling it gracefully and constructively can significantly impact client relationships and project outcomes.

**Active Listening:** When clients provide feedback, listen actively. Understand their concerns and suggestions fully before responding. This shows respect for their input and demonstrates that you value their perspective.

**Constructive Responses:** Respond to feedback constructively. If a client suggests a change you believe won't work, explain your reasoning and offer alternative solutions. This collaborative approach fosters mutual respect and often leads to better outcomes.

**Example:** A design team working on a mobile app receives feedback from the client that the colour scheme doesn't match their brand identity. Instead of dismissing the feedback, the team explains the design choices and suggests adjustments that align better with the client's brand while maintaining the app's usability. This approach addresses the client's concerns and enhances the design.

## Time Management

Time is one of our most precious resources. Effective time management allows you to complete projects efficiently, meet deadlines, and maintain a healthy work-life balance.

### Prioritisation and Planning

Prioritising tasks and planning your schedule are fundamental to effective time management. Use techniques like the Eisenhower Matrix to categorise tasks based on their urgency and importance.

## The Eisenhower Matrix Framework

The Eisenhower Matrix helps prioritise tasks by categorising them into four quadrants:

### The Eisenhower Matrix Framework

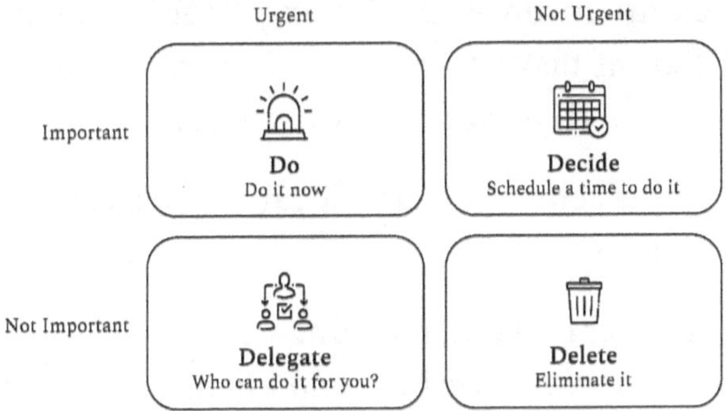


**Urgent and Important:** Tasks that need immediate attention.

**Necessary but Not Urgent:** Tasks that are important for long-term goals but can be scheduled.

**Urgent but Not Important:** Tasks that require immediate attention but do not contribute to long-term goals.

**Not Urgent and Not Important:** Tasks that are distractions and should be minimised.

**Example:** A freelance designer might use the Eisenhower Matrix to organise daily tasks. For example:

**Urgent and Important:** Finalising a client presentation that is due tomorrow.

**Necessary but Not Urgent:** Working on portfolio updates.

**Urgent but Not Important:** Responding to non-critical emails.

**Not Urgent and Not Important:** Browsing social media.

## Time Blocking Framework

Time blocking involves dedicating specific blocks of time to different tasks or projects. This technique helps minimise distractions and improve focus.

Create a weekly schedule that allocates blocks of time for various activities:

A designer might block mornings for focused design work, afternoons for meetings and emails, and evenings for professional development. By adhering to this schedule, they can ensure that each aspect of their business receives attention.

- **Morning Block:** Client work (9:00 AM - 12:00 PM)

- **Afternoon Block:** Business development (1:00 PM - 3:00 PM)

- **Evening Block:** Skill development and learning (4:00 PM - 6:00 PM)

## Using Productivity Tools

Productivity tools can streamline workflows, manage tasks, and track time. Tools like Trello, Asana, and Toggl can help designers stay organised and productive.

## Example: Using Trello for Project Management

A designer might use Trello to create boards for different projects, with lists for tasks such as "To Do," "In Progress," and "Completed." This visual organisation helps track progress and manage multiple projects simultaneously.

## Intellectual Property Rights

Intellectual property (IP) rights protect the ownership of creative work. Designers should understand their IP rights and ensure that they retain ownership of their work or negotiate fair terms when transferring rights to clients. IP rights can include copyrights, trademarks, and patents.

### Copyright

Copyrights protect designers' original works, granting them exclusive rights to control the use and distribution of their creations. Designers can leverage copyrights to safeguard their artwork, illustrations, digital designs, and more.

**Example:** A graphic designer creates a series of original illustrations for a children's book.

**Use of Copyright:** The designer automatically owns the copyright to these illustrations, allowing them to control who can reproduce, distribute, or create derivative works. If a publishing company wants to use the illustrations for a new book or merchandise, they must obtain permission from the designer, often involving a licensing agreement or royalty payments.

## Trademarks

Trademarks protect brand elements such as logos, names, and slogans, which are crucial for building brand identity and recognition. Designers can help clients create and protect these brand elements, ensuring they are distinct and legally safeguarded.

**Example:** A designer develops a comprehensive brand identity package for a new product line, including a unique name and visual elements.

**Use of Trademark:** The client registers the brand name and visual elements as trademarks, safeguarding their brand identity. This legal protection helps maintain the brand's integrity and prevents other companies from using similar names or designs that could dilute the brand's value.

## Patents

Design patents protect a product's ornamental aspects, allowing designers to secure their innovative designs against copying and misuse. While utility patents cover functional features, design patents focus on aesthetic qualities.

### Patents in Product Design

**Example:** A designer creates an innovative chair with a unique shape and decorative elements.

**Use of Design Patent:** The designer files for a design patent to protect the chair's visual appearance. If a competitor tries to produce a similar-looking chair, the designer can enforce their patent rights to prevent imitation and ensure their design remains exclusive.

**Consumer Goods:**

**Example:** A designer develops a new smartphone case with a distinctive pattern and form.

**Use of Design Patent:** The designer obtains a design patent for the smartphone case, protecting its unique appearance. This prevents other manufacturers from producing identical or similar cases, ensuring that the designer's product stands out in the market.

By understanding and utilising different types of intellectual property—copyrights, trademarks, and patents—designers can effectively protect their creative work and enhance their professional practice. These tools provide legal safeguards that allow designers to control the use of their designs, maintain brand integrity, and secure their innovative ideas against unauthorised use. Leveraging intellectual property rights ensures that designers can focus on creativity and innovation, confident that their work is legally protected.

## Conclusion

In this chapter, we explored the intricate balance between creativity and commerce in the design industry. Understanding business goals and aligning design strategies with them is crucial for success. Effective pricing, strong client relationships, managing IP, and financial literacy empower designers to navigate the commercial aspects of their work, ensuring profitability and sustainable growth. By mastering these principles, designers can enhance their impact, drive innovation, and build thriving, successful businesses.

# Quick Recap: The Infinite Canvas of Creativity

As we conclude this journey through the realms of design, it is important to reflect on the profound insights and transformative lessons shared by the visionaries we've encountered. Each chapter of this book has been a brushstroke, adding depth, colour, and texture to the infinite canvas of creativity that defines the design world.

Design is more than a profession; it is a calling that demands passion, resilience, empathy, and an unwavering commitment to innovation. From the fundamental principles that ground us to the cutting-edge technologies that propel us forward, the field of design offers endless possibilities for those willing to explore its vast landscape.

**Embracing the Heart of Empathy**

Empathy is the cornerstone of meaningful design. By understanding the diverse experiences, needs, and emotions of others, we can create solutions that truly resonate. As designers, our ability to step into the shoes of our users, clients, and communities enables us to craft experiences that are not only functional but also profoundly human.

**Nodes of Wisdom**

Remember, every interaction, feedback, and story shared is an opportunity to learn and grow. Let empathy guide your design process and illuminate your path forward.

## Crafting Compelling Narratives

Storytelling is the art of breathing life into data and transforming insights into impactful narratives. Through storytelling, we connect with our audience, convey our vision, and inspire action. Whether presenting a design concept, pitching to a client, or sharing your work with the world, remember that your story is as important as the design itself.

Harness the power of narratives to make your work memorable, to evoke emotions, and to drive meaningful change. Let your designs tell stories that matter.

## Mastering the Fundamentals

The timeless fundamentals of design are the bedrock upon which all innovation is built. Mastering the basics gives you the confidence and skill to push boundaries and explore new frontiers. But remember, these fundamentals are not rigid rules; they are guidelines that can be bent, twisted, and even broken when creativity demands it.

As you continue your journey, keep refining your craft, stay curious, and never stop learning. Mastering design is a lifelong pursuit.

## Unleashing Curiosity

Curiosity is the spark that ignites creativity. It is the relentless pursuit of knowledge, the eagerness to explore the unknown, and the courage to ask "what if." Embrace your curiosity and let it lead you to uncharted territories. Every question, every experiment, and every failure is a stepping stone towards discovery.

In a world that is constantly evolving, curiosity is your greatest ally. Let it drive your innovation and fuel your passion.

## Building Your Legacy

Your personal brand is your legacy. It is the reflection of your values, your expertise, and your unique perspective. As you build your brand, strive for authenticity, integrity, and excellence. Share your journey, connect with others, and contribute to the community.

Remember, your brand is what you do and who you are. Let it be a testament to your dedication, creativity and impact.

## Stand up and face defeat.

Resilience is the strength to rise after every fall, learn from every setback, and persevere in adversity. The design journey is fraught with challenges, but it is through these challenges that we grow and evolve.

Embrace failure as part of the process and let each obstacle be a lesson. Your resilience will shape your career and define your character.

## The Gift of Feedback

Feedback is a powerful tool for growth and improvement. Constructive criticism refines our designs and elevates our work. Learn to embrace feedback with an open mind and a willingness to learn. Provide feedback with empathy and respect and foster a culture of continuous improvement.

Feedback is not a judgement; it is a gift. Use it to become a better designer and a better person.

## Leading with Purpose

Design leadership is about inspiring and guiding others to create meaningful work. It is about fostering a culture of innovation, collaboration, and integrity. As a design leader, your role is to empower your team, cultivate their talents and drive a shared vision.

Lead with purpose, and let your values guide your decisions. Your leadership will shape the future of design.

## The Intersection of Art and Design

Art and design often intersect, creating a dynamic creative landscape. Artistic principles can enhance design practice, offering new perspectives and techniques. Interdisciplinary collaboration between artists and designers can lead to innovative and unexpected results.

Embrace the fluid boundaries between art and design. Let the principles of art inspire your work and broaden your creative horizons.

## Designing Beyond Screens

Design is not confined to digital screens. Physical products, spatial experiences, and environmentally responsible designs are crucial in shaping our interactions with the world. By considering the broader context, designers can create holistic and impactful experiences.

Think beyond screens. Consider how your designs interact with the physical world and contribute to sustainable practices.

## The Art and Science of Data-Driven Design

Data is a powerful tool for informing design decisions. Integrating data into your design process can provide valuable insights, optimise designs, and create impactful visualisations. Use data to drive deeper understanding and innovation.

Leverage data as a design tool. Let it inform your decisions and enhance the effectiveness of your work.

## AI and the Creative Process

Artificial Intelligence is revolutionising the design industry. AI can enhance creativity, offer new tools, and provide practical applications in design. Ethical considerations and practical frameworks are essential for integrating AI into the creative process.

Embrace AI as a collaborator. Use it to augment your creativity and explore new possibilities.

## Immersive Realities: AR, VR, and Intelligent Interfaces

AR, VR, and intelligent interfaces transform how we interact with digital and physical spaces. These technologies offer new opportunities for creativity, innovation, and engagement. They represent the next frontier in design.

Explore immersive realities. Harness the power of AR, VR, and intelligent interfaces to create transformative experiences.

## Designing for All

Inclusivity and accessibility are at the heart of ethical design. Creating experiences that are accessible to everyone ensures no one is left behind. Advocacy for inclusivity and designing with empathy are paramount.

Design for all. Create inclusive experiences that empower and engage every user.

## The Business of Design: Balancing Creativity and Commerce

Understanding how to balance creativity with commerce is crucial for any designer aiming for long-term success. It involves aligning design work with business goals, mastering various pricing strategies, and enhancing financial literacy. This underscores the importance of building and maintaining strong client relationships while integrating design seamlessly into broader business strategies. By following practical frameworks and learning from real-world examples, designers can ensure sustainable growth, drive innovation, and achieve profitability in their creative endeavours.

# Conclusion: Designing the Future Together

As we reach the end of this journey, I extend my heartfelt thanks to each of you. Your dedication to the craft of design, your willingness to learn and grow, and your passion for creativity are what drive this field forward.

We've explored the heart of empathy, the power of storytelling, the importance of mastering fundamentals, and the endless potential of emerging technologies. But more importantly, we've discovered that the essence of great design lies in our ability to connect, inspire, and make a difference.

The future of design is bright and filled with possibilities. Emerging technologies like AR, VR, and AI are opening new horizons, while principles of accessibility and inclusivity are ensuring that our designs touch every corner of society. As you move forward, remember that you have the power to shape this future.

Embrace your curiosity, build your personal brand, and lead with purpose—design with empathy, resilience, and a commitment to inclusivity. Let your work tell stories that inspire and create experiences that resonate deeply with those who interact with them.

I challenge you to apply what you've learned in ways that push the boundaries of creativity and innovation. Share your journey, collaborate with others, and contribute to the vibrant community of designers worldwide.

Thank you for joining me on this journey. Together, we can create a world where design is seen and felt, every interaction is meaningful, and creativity knows no bounds.

Keep designing. Keep dreaming. Keep creating.

With gratitude and inspiration,
Tejj

# Acknowledgements

This book is the result of an incredible journey that began over five years ago with the creation of the Nodes of Design podcast. It has been a labour of love, filled with countless hours of conversation, reflection, and learning. I am deeply grateful to everyone who has been a part of this journey.

First and foremost, I extend my heartfelt thanks to all the guests who generously shared their time, insights, and experiences on the podcast. Your stories and wisdom have enriched the podcast and become the foundation of this book. Thank you for your openness, inspiration, and invaluable contributions—guests on the podcasts in the sequences of the latest episode at the time of writing.

Wolfgang Bremer, Gloria Osardu Ph.D, Aditi Sharma, Ruki Neuhold-Ravikumar, Karen Korellis Reuther, Connor Moore, Jakob Nielsen, Andy Budd, Albert Shum, Gordon Ching, Kirti Trivedi, Anton Stén, Alexander Christian, Rachel Kobetz, Don Norman, Deepak Menon, Christopher Reardon, Guthrie Dolin, Anab Jain,, Matthew Holloway, Sheri Panabaker, Irene Au, Darjan Hil, Amit Dangwal, Nicole Lachenmeier, Ryan Rumsey, Kristen Shenk, Susan Weinschenk PhD, Iain McConchie, Rafael Brandão, Denise Pilar, Bob Baxley, Charles L

**Nodes of Wisdom**

Mauro CHFP, Reggie Murphy Ph.D, Eva Deckers, Nur Karadeniz, Rich McCoy, Afshin Mehin, Brigette Metzler, Kieron Lewis, Randy Herbertson, Ashwin Rajan, Varun, June Mineyama-Smithson, R. Michael Hendrix, Craig Black, Nancy Kumar, Steve Portigal, Ekta Rohra Jafri, Roberta Virzi, Claudio Baptista, Jason Forrest, Steve Bromley, Eric L Hu, Joe Stitzlein, Ricardo Martins, Tejo Guna, Brittney Mills Ph.D, Sydney Hardy, Lex Roman, Lily Konings, Shiva Jaini, Florian van Schreven, Janel Torkington, Aleksandra Artamonovskaja, Derek Mei, Christopher Riggs, Tom Ross and Michael Janda, Paige Bennett, Riya Thosar, Crystal Sundaramoorthy, Janaki Kumar, Phil Balagtas, Camila Nogueira, Jonathan Javier, Amy Wang, Jonathan Even-Zohar, Parag Trivedi, Phillip J. Clayton, Yomar Augusto, Michael Janda, Pradeep Nayar, Matt Clack, Lijo Joseph, Gabriele Romagnoli, Aaron Breuer, Jason Blackheart, Akshay Kore, Guru Vaidya, Pål Eirik Paulsen, Dr.Kirell Benzi, Tanushree Bishnoi, Manuel Lima, Amit Patil, Ana Santos, Saurabh Srivastava, Maitreyee Kalaskar, Paavan Buddhdev, Sharif Matar, Fabin Rasheed, Nelio Barros, Nikhil Pawar, Patricia Reiners, Elize Todd, Luis Ouriach, Eric Lauer, Miriam Isaac, Alex Dovhyi, Blesson Varghese, Romina Hakim, Dot Lung, Daniel Patterson, Krishna Kishore Pande, Radhika Jamwal.

A special thank you to Amit Patil, whose unwavering support and encouragement inspired me to take the leap and write a book. Your support has been a constant source of motivation, and I am truly grateful for your friendship and guidance.

I want to extend my heartfelt gratitude to Wolfgang Bremer, Gloria Osardu, Rafael Brandão, Iain McConchie, Riya Thosar, Denise Pilar, Amit Patil, Manuel Lima, Anton Sten, Rich McCoy, Sharif Matar, Kristen Shenk, Ruki Neuhold-Ravikumar and Ekta Rohra Jafri each of you for taking the time to read 'Nodes of Wisdom: Lessons from 100 Creative Visionaries.' Your invaluable feedback and support have been instrumental in shaping the book into what it is today. Your insights, reflections, and encouragement have added immense value, and I am deeply thankful for your support to this book.

I want to thank the early readers, Bhaskar Komara, Sravani Rasineni, Lakshmi Misra, Rohit Sai, Margi Kapadia and Parikshit.

To my listeners, who have been the driving force behind this endeavour, thank you for your enthusiasm, feedback, and persistent requests for a distilled version of the podcast. This book is for you, a tangible guide to carry along and refer to on your design journey.

To my family, thank you for your endless support and love. Your belief in me has been my anchor and my greatest strength.

And finally, to everyone who has prayed for me, blessed me, and sent positive thoughts my way, your kindness has been the invisible hand guiding me through every challenge and triumph.

This book is a testament to the power of community, the importance of sharing knowledge, and the incredible journey of learning and growth. Thank you all for being a part of this journey. Upwards and Onwards.

Please take a moment to review my book on Amazon, Goodreads, or any other platform where you found it. If you have any questions, comments, edits, or feedback, please email me at design.tejj@gmail.com

# A Simple Design Reflection Worksheet

- Who is the primary user of this design? (Think about their demographics, needs, and preferences)

- What problem does this design solve? (Identify the core issue or pain point it addresses)

- How does this design improve the user's experience? (Consider usability, functionality, and emotional impact.)

- What are the core principles guiding this design? (List the fundamental design principles you adhered to)

- What emotions should the design evoke? (Describe the feelings you aim to inspire in the user)

- How does this design reflect your unique style? (Identify elements that showcase your personal design touch)

- What sustainability considerations were made? (Discuss efforts to ensure the design is environmentally friendly)

- What story does this design tell? (Outline the narrative or message conveyed through the design)

- What feedback have you received on this design? (Summarise key insights and critiques from users or peers)

- How have you iterated on this design based on feedback? ( Describe changes made to improve the design)

- What impact has this design had on its users? (Provide evidence or anecdotes of its effectiveness)

- What challenges did you face during the design process? (Reflect on obstacles and how you overcame them)

- What tools and techniques did you use in this design? (List software, methodologies, or practices employed)

- How does this design integrate with other systems or products? (Explain its compatibility and interaction with existing solutions)

- How will this design evolve in the future? (Consider potential updates or improvements)

- What did you learn from this design project? (Reflect on personal and professional growth)

- Are you proud of this design? Why or why not? (Evaluate your satisfaction with the final product)

# Share the Insights

Who else can benefit from this book? Make a list of peers or colleagues you believe would gain valuable insights from this book. Add a few names, and then pass it on (cross yourself off the list before you do).

# Appendix

**Empathy and Storytelling**

- Empathy
- Empathy Mapping
- Case Study: Designing with Empathy
- Cultivating Empathy
- Storytelling
- Design Narratives
- Portfolio Storytelling
- Engaging Narratives

**Fundamentals and Innovation**

- Design Fundamentals
- Frameworks for Mastering Fundamentals
- Timeless Principles
- Rule-Breaking
- Curiosity
- Growth Mindset
- Lifelong Learning
- Innovation

**Mentorship**

- Finding the Right Mentors
- Building Supportive Communities

**Nodes of Wisdom**

- Networking
- Impact of Mentorship

## Community Building

- Importance of Community
- Building a Network
- Engaging with Peers
- Community Impact on Growth

## Resilience

- Building Resilience
- Learning from Failure
- Consistency
- Overcoming Challenges

## Feedback

- Embracing Feedback
- Providing Constructive Criticism
- Incorporating Feedback
- Shaping Design with Feedback

## Data-Driven Design

- Integrating Data into Design
- Creating Impactful Visualisations
- Leveraging Data Insights
- Case Study: Data-Driven Success

## Technology in Design

- AI in Design
- Ethical Considerations of AI

- Practical AI Applications
- AI-Driven Design Projects

## Physical Design

- Designing Physical Products
- Spatial Experiences
- Environmental Responsibility
- Physical Design Case Studies

## Art in Design

- Enhancing Design with Art
- Interdisciplinary Collaboration
- Lessons from Art History
- Art-Driven Design Innovations

## Personal Branding

- Importance of Personal Branding
- Building an Authentic Brand
- Practical Branding Tips
- Successful Designer Brands

## Accessibility in Design

- Principles of Accessible Design
- Frameworks for Inclusive Design
- Benefits of Accessibility
- Case Studies in Inclusive Design

## Immersive Realities

- The potential of AR and VR
- Advancements in Intelligent Interfaces

## Design and Business Integration

- Integrating Design with Business Goals
- Positioning Design as a Strategic Asset
- Case Studies in Design-Driven Business Success

# Nodes of Design Podcast

"Nodes of Design" is a platform dedicated to exploring the diverse world of design and art through conversations with top creatives. Its mission is to inspire, educate, and connect designers from all backgrounds. Through insightful interviews, it offers a glimpse into the minds of visionary creatives, sharing their processes, challenges, and successes. Whether a novice or a seasoned professional, Nodes of Design Podcast is your go-to source for inspiration, learning, and connecting with the global design community.

**Nodes of Wisdom**

It is also one of the first India's design podcasts featuring multiple global creative leaders to reach powerful platforms like Google Podcast, Apple Podcast, Amazon Music, and Spotify; the Podcast is available on eight other streaming platforms with listeners from 60 countries across the globe. Topping the Apple Podcast charts in the design & art category at #1 in over ten countries like India, Hungary, Denmark, Romania, Pakistan, Azerbaijan, Philippines, Nigeria, Lithuania, and Thailand and in the top 10 podcasts charts in over 30 countries

## Newsletter: The Creative Note

Stay inspired and ahead of the curve! Subscribe to our newsletter for exclusive insights, updates, tips on AI, creative trends, and much more delivered straight to your inbox.

Sign up at https://thecreativee.substack.com or scan the QR code below.

# About the Author

Ravi Tejj is an award-winning product designer renowned for his innovative solutions spanning various industries, from Fortune 500 companies to dynamic startups. Currently, Tejj is making significant strides at Microsoft AI, where he is dedicated to designing health experiences on Windows and the Web.

Beyond his professional accomplishments, Tejj has a profound impact on the design community. He has mentored over 300+ creatives and has been recognised as one of the Top 1% of Design Mentors globally on ADPList, helping shape the next generation of designers. With his Design with Tejj YouTube channel, he has significantly impacted design education by assisting aspirants to secure ranks and admissions in top design schools worldwide.

Tejj is also the esteemed host of the globally acclaimed 'Nodes of Design' and 'Product Unwind' podcasts, which explore the frontiers of design and product management. He is also the founder of the creativee community, a global community for creatives.

He has spoken on prominent stages and podcasts, including the UXDG Conference, Microsoft Design Week, Adplist, and Art+Heritage at Salarjung Museum, among many others. Tejj's contributions are shaping the future of design and inspiring a whole new generation of designers and creatives worldwide.